Project Plan—Surficial Geologic Mapping and Hydrogeologic Framework Studies in the Greater Platte River Basins (Central Great Plains) in Support of Ecosystem and Climate Change Research

By Margaret E. Berry, Scott C. Lundstrom, Janet L. Slate, Daniel R. Muhs, David A. Sawyer, and Darren R. Van Sistine

Open-File Report 2011–1010

U. S. Department of the Interior
U. S. Geological Survey

U. S. Department of the Interior
KEN SALAZAR, Secretary

U. S. Geological Survey
Marcia K. McNutt, Director

U. S. Geological Survey, Reston, Virginia 2011

For product and ordering information:
World Wide Web: http://www. usgs. gov/pubprod
Telephone: 1-888-ASK-USGS

For more information on the USGS—the Federal source for science about the Earth,
its natural and living resources, natural hazards, and the environment:
World Wide Web: http://www. usgs. gov
Telephone: 1-888-ASK-USGS

Contents

Figures

Acronyms

CEN	Climate Effects Network
CGGSC	Crustal Geophysics and Geochemistry Science Center
CGS	Colorado Geological Survey
CSD	Conservation and Survey Division
GECSC	Geology and Environmental Change Science Center
GPRB	Greater Platte River Basins
KGS	Kansas Geological Survey
KSWSC	Kansas Water Science Center
NCGMP	National Cooperative Geologic Mapping Program
NEWSC	Nebraska Water Science Center
NIOB	Niobrara National Scenic River
NPS	National Park Service
NRD	Nebraska Natural Resource Districts
UNL	University of Nebraska-Lincoln
USGS	U.S. Geological Survey
ka	kilo-annum, 10^3 years

Project Plan—Surficial Geologic Mapping and Hydrogeologic Framework Studies in the Greater Platte River Basins (Central Great Plains) in Support of Ecosystem and Climate Change Research

By Margaret E. Berry, Scott C. Lundstrom, Janet L. Slate, Daniel R. Muhs, David A. Sawyer, and Darren R. Van Sistine

Abstract

Geologic mapping studies are underway to help define the geologic framework for integrated ecosystem and climate change research in the Greater Platte River Basins, an ecoregion being targeted for collaborative observation and research by the Climate Effects Network (CEN) of the U.S. Geological Survey (USGS) Global Change Program. Geologic mapping and associated geochronological research provide information about physical and chemical properties, distribution, age, origin, and stratigraphic relations of surficial geologic deposits for reconstructing geologic and hydrologic history and for recognizing geomorphic response to climate change that is recorded in the geologic record.

Planned surficial geologic mapping and research under the new "Greater Platte River Basins and Northern Plains Geologic Framework Studies Project" primarily focuses on three areas: (1) the South Platte River on the drought-prone eastern plains of Colorado, a semiarid environment where geomorphic systems tend to be highly sensitive to climate change; (2) the Niobrara National Scenic River in northern Nebraska, situated at the crossroads of several ecosystems, where many plant and animal species are near the limits of their usual geographic range, and geomorphic systems may be near threshold limits; and (3) the Crescent Lake Wildlife Refuge area in the western Nebraska Sand Hills, where dune migration during past episodes of eolian sand activity blocked stream drainages and created numerous lakes. In each of these areas, the geologic records of fluvial and eolian systems are intimately connected and reflective of past climate change. Large-scale geologic mapping in these areas, which will complement ongoing studies by other researchers, will lead to a better understanding of how climate change has affected the geomorphic systems in the past, and how it might affect them in the future. This information is vital to preserving and sustaining healthy human and wildlife habitats, adequate water supplies, and operational infrastructure.

Planned hydrogeologic framework studies under the new "Greater Platte River Basins and Northern Plains Geologic Framework Studies Project" focus primarily on groundwater issues in a fourth area, the Republican River drainage of southern Nebraska and northern Kansas. Sustainability of water in the basin has been a key topic of concern between states sharing the water supply, a concern intensified by the possibility of further diminishing water resources as climate changes. New digital geologic mapping of selected areas will improve understanding of the complex geologic framework that affects groundwater flow and groundwater-surface water interactions in and around the basin, and help address the major issue of water sustainability.

Introduction

The Greater Platte River Basins (GPRB; Thormodsgard, 2009) area spans a central part of the midcontinent and Great Plains from the Rocky Mountains on the west to the Missouri River on the east, and is defined to include drainage areas of the Platte, Niobrara, and Republican Rivers, the Rainwater Basin (LaGrange, 2005), and other adjoining areas overlying the northern High Plains aquifer (fig. 1). The GPRB contains abundant surficial deposits that were sensitive to, or are reflective of, the climate under which they formed: deposits from multiple glaciations in the mountain headwaters of the North and South Platte Rivers and from continental ice sheets in eastern Nebraska; fluvial terraces (ranging from Tertiary to Holocene in age) along the rivers and streams; vast areas of eolian sand in the Nebraska Sand Hills and other dune fields (recording multiple episodes of dune activity); thick sequences of windblown silt (loess); and sediment deposited in numerous lakes and wetlands (Swinehart and others, 1994; Soller and others, 2009). In addition, the GPRB overlies and contributes surface water to the High Plains aquifer, a nationally important groundwater system that underlies parts of eight states and sustains one of the major agricultural areas of the United States (Weeks and others, 1988; Luckey and others, 1988; McMahon and others, 2007). The area also provides critical nesting habitat for birds such as plovers and terns, and roosting habitat for cranes and other migratory birds that travel through the Central Flyway of North America (Committee on Endangered and Threatened Species in the Platte River Basin, National Research Council, 2004; http://flyways.us/flyways/info). This broad area, containing fragile ecosystems that could be further threatened by changes in climate and land use, has been identified by the USGS and the University of Nebraska-Lincoln as a region where intensive collaborative research could lead to a better understanding of climate change and what might be done to adapt to or mitigate its adverse effects to ecosystems and to humans (University of Nebraska-Lincoln Office of Research, 2008). The need for robust data on the geologic framework of ecosystems in the GPRB has been acknowledged in proceedings from the 2008 Climate Change Workshop (University of Nebraska-Lincoln Office of Research, 2008) and in draft reports by researchers developing a multidisciplinary science plan for the GPRB.

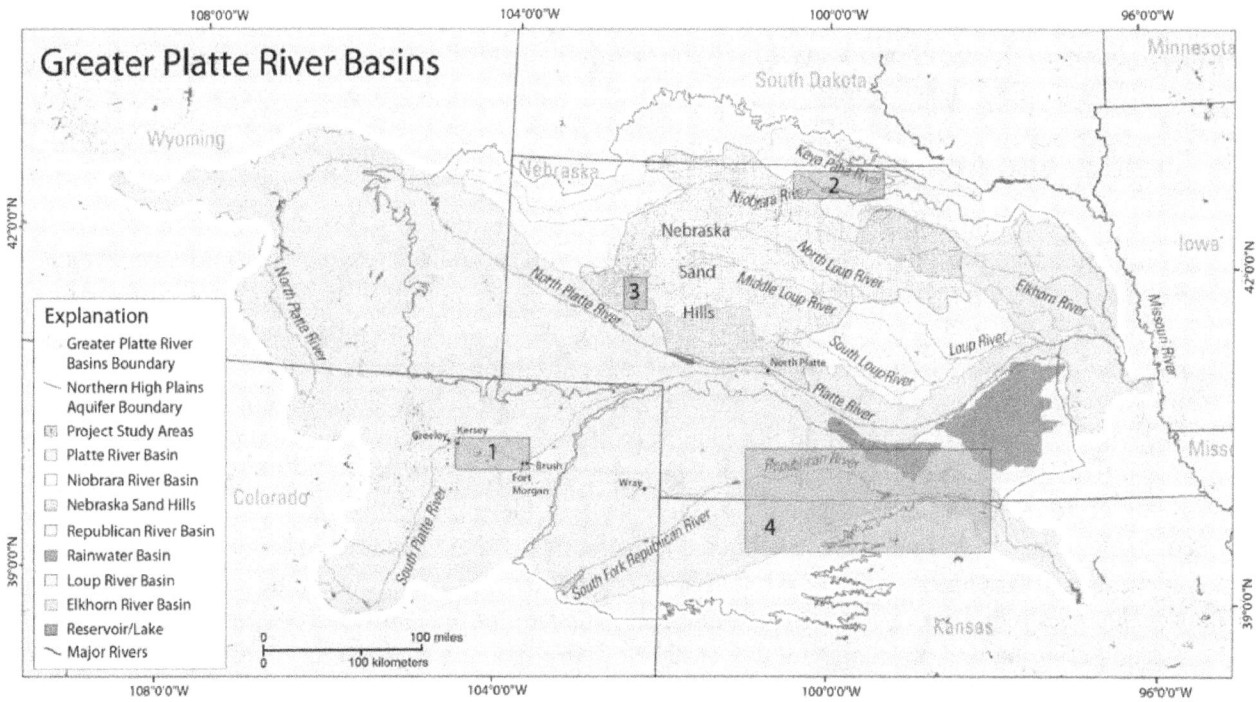

Figure 1. Map showing the Greater Platte River Basins, northern part of the High Plains aquifer, and general study areas targeted for this project: (1) South Platte River corridor, (2) Niobrara National Scenic River, (3) Crescent Lake Wildlife Refuge area, and (4) Republican River area. Eolian sediments cover much of the GPRB although only the Nebraska Sand Hills are shown here. Base map taken from Thormodsgard (2009).

Project Objectives

The USGS Geology and Environmental Change Science Center (GECSC) has initiated surficial geologic mapping and hydrogeologic framework studies in the GPRB in support of ecosystem and climate change research ("Greater Platte River Basins and Northern Plains Geologic Framework Studies Project"); these studies are funded chiefly by the USGS National Cooperative Geologic Mapping Program (NCGMP; *http://ncgmp.usgs.gov/*), with supplemental contributions from the USGS Global Change Program (*http://www.usgs.gov/global_change/*). The overall objective of these studies is to help define the geologic framework of ecosystems in the GPRB by providing information about physical properties, geochemistry, stratigraphic relations, age, origin, and areal distribution of geologic mapping units. Goals are to obtain a better understanding of (1) past climate information recorded in the geologic record, and (2) geomorphic or climatic thresholds that may have triggered major changes in the ecosystems in the past. This information will be vital to regional land-use decision makers and managers trying to anticipate effects of future climate change and make informed choices among competing land uses.

Our goal has been to develop this project in partnership with the USGS Global Change Program, and to collaborate with other agencies and academia conducting research in the GPRB. This project directly supports the USGS Science Strategy by evaluating past interactions between climate, earth surface processes, and ecosystems (relevant to understanding ecosystem sustainability, and wildlife and human health), and generating new information for modeling aquifer systems that can be used to manage and protect drinking-water supplies. The project also will be relevant to addressing natural hazards, through identification of floods and wildfires recorded in the geologic record and assessing mineral and aggregate resources.

Strategy and Approach

Preliminary objectives of this project have been to identify key areas where new surficial geologic mapping and hydrogeologic framework studies could address paleoclimate, ecosystem, and/or groundwater-related issues within the GPRB. As a result of numerous meetings and discussions with collaborators, assessing the current state of geologic mapping (Appendix) and other relevant geologic data, and conducting field reconnaissance, we have identified three study areas for new, detailed surficial geologic mapping subtasks that will address major ecosystem and climate change issues: (1) the South Platte River corridor on the eastern plains of Colorado; (2) the Niobrara National Scenic River, transecting the northern Sand Hills in Nebraska; and (3) the Crescent Lake Wildlife Refuge area, in the western Nebraska Sand Hills (fig. 1). In each of these areas, the geologic records of fluvial and eolian systems are intimately interrelated and reflective of past changes in climate. Large-scale geologic mapping will emphasize river floodplain and terrace deposits; sand dune, interdune, and dune-dammed lake deposits; windblown silt deposits, and relations among these different types of surficial deposits, and will complement ongoing studies by other researchers in a multiple of disciplines. In addition, the mapping will identify areas of the landscape susceptible to sediment or soil erosion, which affects soil productivity, sediment load in streams and lakes, water quality, and fish and wildlife habitat, and can lead to future collaboration with biologists working in the GPRB.

These surficial geologic mapping subtasks of our NCGMP project are being developed in an integrated fashion with the "Impacts of Climate Change on Coastal and Eolian Landscapes Project" (funded by the USGS Office of Global Change) through a joint subtask entitled "Eolian Sediments in the Greater Platte River Basins, Great Plains." One objective of the eolian sediments subtask is to understand the dynamics of sand dune formation and activity in the GPRB. A second objective is to infer past climates from loess (windblown silt) records and compare results with general circulation models.

In addition, the Republican River area of southern Nebraska and northern Kansas (fig. 1) has been identified as a watershed where hydrogeologic framework studies could help address critical issues concerning water sustainability in the basin. New digital geologic mapping of selected areas will improve understanding of the complex geologic framework that affects groundwater flow and groundwater-surface water interactions in and around the basin, and lead to a better understanding of how best to model and manage the groundwater resources.

Surficial Geologic Mapping Studies

Methodology

Objectives of the surficial geologic mapping task will be addressed through large-scale (generally 1:24,000) digital geologic mapping, sedimentologic, and stratigraphic studies (aided by drilling or backhoe excavation where appropriate and feasible) of surficial geologic materials using a combination of field, remote sensing, geochronology and other laboratory techniques, and incorporating geophysical, well, or other subsurface data where available. Geochronology will be established through dating (primarily radiocarbon and luminescence methods), tephrochronolgy, geoarchaeology, and paleontology where applicable. Surface soils, paleosols, and peat deposits will be described and sampled for relative age assessment, radiocarbon dating, and/or inferences about paleoenvironment. For the Crescent Lake Wildlife Refuge area, historical study will be conducted using archival aerial photography and available written records. Digital maps will be published at a scale determined most appropriate to convey significant results.

Communication Plan

This task is being coordinated with other scientific entities, including the USGS Nebraska Water Science Center (NEWSC), the USGS Crustal Geophysics and Geochemistry Science Center (CGGSC), the CEN of the USGS Global Change Program, the University of Nebraska-Lincoln (UNL) Conservation and Survey Division (CSD), several Nebraska Natural Resource Districts (NRD), the National Park Service (NPS), and the Colorado Geological Survey (CGS). Task members will communicate frequently with these agencies about our research activities. Project results will be communicated through a variety of methods: (1) poster or oral presentations at professional meetings; (2) field trips with collaborators and other interested parties; (3) USGS publications (maps, reports, and/or fact sheets); (4) peer-reviewed scientific journal articles or book chapters; (5) a project-Web site, which could be of interest to scientists, stakeholders, and the general public; and, (6) if results warrant it, newspapers or other news media.

Subtask: South Platte River Corridor, Eastern Colorado

For more than half its length, the Platte River system is made up of two rivers, the South and North Platte, both of which have headwaters in the Colorado Rocky Mountains and merge downstream to form the central Platte River near North Platte, Nebraska (fig. 1). The South Platte River flows across the semiarid, short-grass prairie of eastern Colorado, a region highly susceptible to drought (Madole, 1994). Part of the High Plains Ecoregion, the area is higher and drier than areas to the east, with a mean annual precipitation of 12-20 inches (about 30-50 cm) and a mesic temperature regime (Chapman and others, 2006). In this type of semiarid, drought-prone environment, geomorphic systems tend to be highly sensitive to climate change, and surficial deposits provide a past record of system response to that change (for example, Miao and others, 2007). Determining past system response can help predict potential future response to climate change that might have adverse effects on ecosystems and society. The purpose of this subtask is to better understand the fluvial record of the South Platte River on the eastern plains of Colorado, and to relate the record for the South Platte River to records for the North Platte River, central Platte River, and eolian deposits of the GPRB, through collaborative work with other researchers.

Geologic Setting

Nine topographic levels that define the tops of fluvial terraces have been recognized along the South Platte River, including: pre-Rocky Flats alluvium (mapped as Pliocene Nussbaum Alluvium in some studies), early Pleistocene Rocky Flats, early middle Pleistocene Verdos (about 640 thousand years [ka]), middle Pleistocene Slocum, late middle Pleistocene Louviers (thought to be correlative in age to Bull Lake till), and late Pleistocene Broadway (thought to be correlative in age to Pinedale till) Alluviums, and Holocene pre-Piney Creek alluvium, Piney Creek Alluvium, and post-Piney Creek alluvium (Madole, 1991; Lindsey and others, 2005). The presence of additional, less distinct Holocene alluvial units is suggested by data from some archeological sites (Madole, 1991).

In addition to fluvial terraces, multiple generations of eolian silt and sand deposits, generated in part from fluvial sediments of the South Platte River, cover much of the terrain (Madole, 1991, 1995;

Jorgensen, 1992; Forman and others, 1995; Muhs and others, 1996, 1999a, 1999b; Aleinikoff and others, 1999; Madole and others, 2005; Aleinikoff and Muhs, 2010). Although the eolian sand is stabilized currently by vegetation, dune stability probably is near threshold limits under the present climate, and therefore slight changes in climate or land use could result in future widespread eolian sand transport (Madole, 1994; Muhs and Maat, 1993; Muhs and Holliday, 1995).

Mapping and Research Plan

Recent geologic mapping efforts in the South Platte drainage have focused on the mountainous headwaters and the urban corridor along the Colorado Front Range (Appendix). Aside from geoarchaeological and pedologic work on late Pleistocene and Holocene terraces near Kersey, Colorado (Holliday, 1987; McFaul and others, 1994; Muhs and others, 1996), little geologic mapping and research on fluvial deposits has been done along the South Platte River corridor downstream from Greeley, Colorado, since the seminal work of Glenn Scott on the Sterling 1° x 2° quadrangle (Scott, 1978; 1982). Much remains to be learned about the fluvial history for this part of the river. Our objectives are to map, characterize, and develop a geochronology and stratigraphy for surficial deposits along a portion of the South Platte River corridor in eastern Colorado. Our work will build on research recently published on Quaternary alluvial deposits of the South Platte River and tributaries in the urban corridor region west of the study area (Lindsey and others, 2005), new geologic mapping in the mountains and urban corridor along the Front Range (Kellogg and others, 2008; Cole and Braddock, 2009; mapping in progress, Appendix), and older geologic mapping within the study area (Greeley 1° x 2° quadrangle, Braddock and Cole, 1978; Sterling 1° x 2° quadrangle, Scott, 1978, 1982; Orchard, Weldona, and Fort Morgan 7 1/2' quadrangles, Gardner, 1967). Specific areas for initial mapping and research will be affected by availability of field exposures and land access, but our plan is to focus on the area between Kersey and Brush, Colo. This stretch of river has been affected by past alpine glaciations in the headwaters, and more locally, by past droughts severe enough to mobilize dune sand and produce significant deposits of wind-blown silt in the basin.

This research complements work conducted through STATEMAP (NCGMP's matching-funds grant program with State geological surveys; *http://ncgmp.usgs.gov/ncgmpabout/statemap*) by the UNL CSD on the North Platte and central Platte rivers in Nebraska, for which the fluvial history also is poorly understood. This collaborative strategy will allow us to synthesize a more complete picture of the fluvial history of the Platte River system by producing data for a larger portion of the river basin, filling a significant data gap and strengthening the significance of both FEDMAP (NCGMP's program that funds Federal geologic mapping projects; *http://ncgmp.usgs.gov/ncgmpabout/fedmap*) and STATEMAP results. Our NCGMP project is committed to fostering collaborative STATEMAP-FEDMAP work, and therefore could assist with some mapping on the North Platte/central Platte Rivers in Nebraska if needed. The research also complements work being conducted on eolian sediments in the GPRB, which is being conducted in an integrated fashion as a subtask (described in subtask: Eolian Sediments in the Greater Platte River Basins, Great Plains) under both our NCGMP project and the "Impacts of Climate Change on Coastal and Eolian Landscapes Project" (funded by the USGS Office of Global Change).

Subtask: Niobrara National Scenic River, Nebraska

The Niobrara National Scenic River (NIOB), located in northern Nebraska, is situated at the midcontinental crossroads of several ecosystems (National Park Service, 2007), and is renowned for its biological diversity (Johnsgard, 2007). Climate change has the potential of having significant effect in this ecoregion, where many plant and animal species are near their geographic range limits. Geomorphic systems also may be near threshold limits in this ecoregion, and therefore may be particularly responsive to climate change; river response to climate change has been noted during historic time, when prolonged drought of the 1930s induced changes in river channel width (Buchanan, 1981). For these reasons, the unique setting of the NIOB makes it a prime area for detailed geologic mapping and stratigraphic studies focused on the geologic framework of ecosystems and effects of climate change on the fluvial system. In addition, the NIOB lacks geologic map coverage for the NPS Geologic Resources Inventory (GRI) (Bruce Heise, written commun., 2010), and a GRI scoping meeting attended by NPS and USGS staff, held in August 2008, identified better quality geologic map coverage as a need for the NIOB.

Geologic Setting

The NIOB is a 76-mile stretch of river situated at the northern edge of the Nebraska Sand Hills, in an area with 18-20 inches (46-51 cm) of mean annual precipitation and a mesic temperature regime (Chapman and others, 2001). The NIOB river corridor contains abundant surficial deposits that reflect the history of the fluvial system. Alexander and others (2010) recognize four groups of fluvial landforms: low flood plains, inundated most years by the annual peak flood; intermediate flood plains, inundated somewhat less frequently by floods caused by winter ice jams; low terraces, 7–11 ft (2–3.4 m) above median annual discharge; and high terraces, greater than 11 ft (>3.4 m) above median annual discharge. Characterization of the entire suite of terraces was not the focus of their research on modern river channel geometry and hydrogeomorphology, so their surveys did not extend across the full width of the valley (Alexander and others, 2010), but terraces ranging as high as 312 ft (95 m) above the valley floor have been reported (Hearty, 1978). A prominent high terrace, associated with fluvial deposits informally referred to as the Connely Flat beds (Jacobs and others, 2007) and considered late Pleistocene in age, is about 175 ft (53 m) above the valley floor (Diffendal and others, 2008). As many as five terraces are preserved at levels lower than this prominent late Pleistocene terrace (Diffendal and others, 2008). Sand dunes bordering the drainage are stabilized by vegetation, but thick sections of Pleistocene lacustrine sediments found to the west of the NIOB are interpreted as having been deposited in dune-dammed lakes (Jacobs and others, 2007), suggesting that past mobilization of the sand dunes has had a significant effect on the fluvial system.

Mapping and Research Plan

Our goals for this subtask are to map the river corridor along the 76-mile reach designated National Scenic River, and to develop a geochronology and stratigraphy for the surficial-geologic deposits, to satisfy NIOB park needs for a better quality geologic map, and to gain an understanding of how future climate change may affect the Niobrara fluvial system and ecosystems. The prominent high terrace (more than 50 m above the valley floor) described as late Pleistocene in age (Diffendal and others, 2008) poses an intriguing question as to what caused the fluvial system to incise so dramatically in the past, and our goal is to understand better the timing and causes of such river response. Our plan is to coordinate with ongoing fluvial-geomorphologic research being done by the USGS NEWSC (Alexander and others, 2009, 2010), as well as borehole and surface geophysical work being done by the USGS NEWSC and local NRDs in support of groundwater modeling. Our work will build on mapping and research recently published for the O'Neill 1° x 2° quadrangle (Diffendal and others, 2008), which covers the eastern half of the NIOB, and will help fill data gaps in geologic mapping in the western half of the NIOB (Appendix).

Subtask: Crescent Lake Wildlife Refuge Area, Nebraska

The Crescent Lake Wildlife Refuge area is located in the western part of the Nebraska Sand Hills, the largest sand sea in North America. Although relatively dry with 17–19 inches (43–48 cm) of mean annual precipitation, a mesic temperature regime, and a mixed-grass prairie vegetation (Chapman and others, 2001), this part of the Sand Hills is characterized by numerous lakes and wetlands interspersed between the dunes that provide critical roosting habitat for cranes and other migratory birds. Many of the lakes are alkaline, and few to no rivers or streams flow through the area. The sand dunes presently are stabilized by vegetation, but it is unknown how close the landscape is to a critical threshold, and how much additional stress it would take to destabilize the dunefield. Reactivation of dunes in the Sand Hills would have serious effects on agricultural lands, grazing lands, wildlife habitats, and infrastructure.

Geologic Setting

The central Great Plains is a region susceptible to severe, long-term drought (Loope and Swinehart, 2000), which is linked to widespread eolian activity (Mason and others, 2004). Eolian activity has occurred several times in the past 10,000 years (1.0–0.7 ka, 4.5–2.3 ka with peaks centered on 3.8 and 2.5 ka, and a sustained period of eolian activity from 9.6 to 6.5 ka; Miao and others, 2007). Although the dune field was reworked extensively a number of times during the Holocene, it is likely that a dune field also was present during the last glacial period (Muhs and others, 1999b; Loope and Swinehart, 2000; Muhs and others, 2000; Bettis and others, 2003; Mason and others, 2004), and possibly earlier than that, based on the mineralogical maturity of its deposits (Muhs and others, 1997). During past episodes of eolian activity, sand dunes of the western Nebraska Sand Hills migrated across the Blue Creek drainage, burying stream channels and creating dune dams that resulted in the formation of numerous shallow lakes and wetlands (Loope and others, 1995; Mason and others, 1997). These lakes have complex water chemistry, reflecting a complex interaction with the groundwater system (Bleed and Ginsberg, 1990). The lakes vary in size and number seasonally and annually in response to precipitation and evaporation rates, but historic accounts indicate that there also have been changes in lake size and number related to longer climate trends during the 1900s (Bleed and Ginsberg, 1990). It may be that episodic climate changes during the Holocene have caused long-term changes in size and number of lakes, and that a record of those changes is preserved in the interdune wetland and lake sediments; for example, an interdune wetland to the north of the Crescent Lake area has yielded a pollen record indicative of late Pleistocene and Holocene climate changes (Swinehart and others, 1996). To understand such a climate signal, an in depth knowledge of the spatial distribution, sedimentology, hydrogeology, and geologic history of the local dune field, and dune-dammed wetlands and lakes is needed (Loope and others, 1995).

Mapping and Research Plan

Work in the Crescent Lake Wildlife Refuge area is being conducted as part of a collaborative project with the USGS CGGSC and USGS NEWSC, whose teams are collecting airborne geophysical data, interpreting the hydrogeologic framework, and planning future groundwater modeling work; the UNL CSD, whose team is collecting cores and age dating sediments along the airborne transects; and the area NRDs, whose staff can provide critical local insight and experience. Our objectives for this subtask are to understand the climate signal recorded in dune, interdune, dune-dammed lake, wetland, and stream deposits in the Crescent Lakes Wildlife Refuge and surrounding area, through detailed geologic mapping, historic comparative photogeologic mapping, and sediment analyses that complement the work being done by collaborators. Because dune migration would have serious effects on agricultural and grazing lands, wildlife habitats, and infrastructure, a key question for the region centers on how close the Nebraska Sand Hills landscape is to a critical threshold, past which stabilizing vegetation cannot be sustained and sand is remobilized. Our research results will help determine past sensitivity of the geomorphic systems, providing critical information for addressing this question.

The mapping area will focus on the Crescent Lakes Wildlife Refuge and adjacent areas primarily to the north, where numerous lakes occupy interdune areas, but the actual area mapped will be affected by land access, available field exposures, preliminary results of geologic and comparative archival photogeologic mapping, and areas selected for data collection by collaborators.

Subtask: Eolian Sediments in the Greater Platte River Basins, Great Plains

The GPRB occupies a large part of the Great Plains of central North America. It is a semiarid region and like most semiarid regions, experiences a wide range of variability in year-to-year precipitation. This makes the region's geomorphic systems highly sensitive to climate changes. Much of the GPRB is covered with eolian sediments (dune sand, sheet sand, and loess) that are stabilized mostly by vegetation. Reactivation of these deposits is a distinct possibility with shifts in the overall moisture balance, because stabilizing vegetation is dependent highly on precipitation. Effects of future reactivation of eolian sand or loess would be high, and would affect grazing land, agricultural land, wildlife habitats, and infrastructure.

Objectives

Eolian sediments in the GPRB are the focus of a subtask, led by Dan Muhs and funded by the USGS Office of Global Change through the "Impacts of Climate Change on Coastal and Eolian Landscapes Project," being conducted in an integrated fashion with our surficial geologic mapping studies. One objective of this subtask is to understand the dynamics of sand dune formation and activity in the GPRB (for example, Muhs and others, 1996, 1997; Muhs and others, 1999b; Muhs and others, 2000). A second objective is to infer past climates from loess (windblown silt) records and compare results with general circulation models (Muhs and others, 1999b, 2008); paleoclimate data are fundamental to understanding future climate change and its potential effect. Loess is widespread in the central United States and contains one of the most complete records of the last glacial period and the Holocene (Mason and others, 2008). Past wind directions are inferred from loess properties, and past vegetation can be inferred from paleosols within loess (Muhs and others, 2008).

Methodology

Eolian studies involve mapping, in the field and on aerial photographs, sampling and dating (radiocarbon and luminescence methods) stratigraphic sections, and collecting and analyzing sediments for provenance (mineralogical, geochemical, and isotopic methods; Muhs and others, 1996, 1999a; Aleinikoff and others, 1999; Aleinikoff and Muhs, 2010). Historical studies of dune fields are based on archival aerial photography and written accounts. Potential source sediments are sampled and compared with dune sand and loess compositions for inferring paleowinds. Paleosols within loess are studied for inferences about past vegetation.

Research Plan

Several studies associated with this subtask currently (2011) are underway. One study involves testing the suitability of fossil land snails for radiocarbon dating by collecting and analyzing snails from independently dated loess sections in Nebraska and eastern Colorado. Fossil land snails are abundant in loess deposits; developing a reliable technique for dating their shells will provide a valuable method for dating loess sections and potentially other fine-grained terrestrial sediments (Pigati and others, 2010). A second study focuses on provenance of the Wray dune field, eastern Colorado, using geochemical analyses of eolian sand units to test the hypothesis that this dune field is derived from the South Platte River (Muhs and others, 1996; Muhs and others, 1999b). A third focuses on isotopic studies of detrital zircons to determine provenance of the Fort Morgan and Greeley dune fields, eastern Colorado. Current results of this latter work show that although the Fort Morgan dune field is derived from the South Platte River, the Greeley dune field to the north is derived from bedrock sources (Aleinikoff and Muhs, 2010). These results indicate that nonfluvial sources for dunes may be more important than previously thought, and have implications for inferring paleowind direction and for interpreting ties between dune sand and dynamics of the fluvial system.

Work on this subtask as an integrated part of the "Greater Platte River Basin and Northern Plains Geologic Framework Studies" project was made possible by funding from the Global Change Program, and its continuation is dependent on continued support from that program.

Communication Plan

Communication about the results of this study are made through several means: (1) peer-reviewed scientific literature, primarily journal articles and book chapters; (2) oral presentation of results at meetings of national and international scientific organizations and ad hoc, topical conferences; (3) USGS professional papers, fact sheets, and Web sites; and (4) the press, including newspaper articles, magazine articles, and books.

Hydrogeologic Framework Studies

Republican River, Nebraska and Kansas

The GPRB contains some of the most productive agricultural areas in the United States, and is greatly dependent on groundwater for irrigation. The area also is an important ecosystem in the Central Flyway of North America, with whooping cranes and other migratory birds passing through and needing protection of their wildlife habitat. Water resources of the Republican River Basin, used intensively for irrigation as well as for drinking water, recreation, and wildlife habitat, are regulated by an interstate compact between Nebraska, Kansas, and Colorado, and are the subject of litigation between the states over claims of over-appropriation and noncompliance (*http://www.republicanrivercompact.org/; http://www.ksda.gov/interstate_water_issues/content/142*). Water sustainability in the basin is a major concern, made more acute by the possibility of diminishing water supplies as climate changes.

Geologic Setting

Principal groundwater resources of the central Great Plains are contained within the High Plains aquifer (Weeks and others, 1988; McMahon and others, 2007), which is a composite of several distinct, but incompletely mapped, hydrogeologic units of Tertiary to Quaternary age. It overlies mostly marine Cretaceous sedimentary rocks, which also contain a major, mostly fluvial nonmarine aquifer (Dakota Sandstone) in central Nebraska and Kansas. The lowermost hydrogeologic unit in the High Plains aquifer is the Miocene Ogallala Formation (Ludvigson and others, 2009; Macfarlane, 2009), a continental sand and gravel aquifer that has been critically overdrawn in much of its southern extent, from Kansas to Oklahoma and Texas (Weeks and others, 1988). The Ogallala aquifer provides much of the base flow within the Republican River watershed because headwaters of the river are on the High Plains of eastern Colorado and Kansas; in contrast to the Platte River, the Republican River is not connected to any montane recharge. Overlying the Ogallala are Pliocene (including the Broadwater Formation in central Nebraska) and Quaternary alluvial sediments that have variable aquifer properties (Condon, 2005; Macfarlane, 2009), but these sediments have not been uniformly mapped in Nebraska and Kansas. Commonly, these units are combined and referred to as "principal aquifer" or undivided High Plains aquifer. In the central reach of the Republican River of Nebraska, the saturated thickness of the High Plains aquifer is generally less than 300 feet (91 m; McMahon and others, 2007), and locally it may be separated from much thicker parts of the aquifer north of the Platte by outcropping bedrock (for example, Miller and others, 1964; Dreeszen and others, 1973). Interestingly, it has been proposed that in this central reach of the Republican River, there may be early and middle Quaternary Platte River paleovalleys buried beneath younger sediments (for example, Swinehart and others, 1994), which may act as groundwater conduits or create important local aquifers.

Mapping and Research Plan

Hydrogeologic framework studies of the Republican River watershed focus on (1) compiling a new generation of surface and subsurface geologic maps in hydrologically significant parts of the Republican River watershed in Nebraska and Kansas, and (2) relating bedrock and surficial deposits to the Greater Platte River watershed and its ecosystems to better understand surface water-groundwater interactions in the aquifer. This work is being developed in collaboration with the USGS NEWSC and the UNL CSD, and will be coordinated with the Kansas Geological Survey (KGS), USGS Kansas Water Science Center (KSWSC), and local NRDs in Nebraska.

Geologic mapping, at a scale of 1:100,000 or smaller, will build upon available published mapping, including: 1:1,000,000-scale regional Quaternary Atlas maps of the Platte River (Swinehart and others, 1994) and Wichita (Denne and others, 1993) quadrangles; 1:250,000-scale bedrock geologic maps of the McCook (Eversoll and others, 1988) and Grand Island (Dreeszen and others, 1973) quadrangles, which show only thickness of Quaternary deposits; 1:50,000-scale geologic maps of Phillips (Johnson and Arbogast, 1993) and Norton Counties, Kansas (in progress; Appendix); and older but good quality, 1:48,000-scale geologic mapping for Franklin, Nuckolls, and Webster counties, Nebraska (Miller and others, 1964). Quaternary tephra samples from Kansas and Nebraska, housed at the USGS in Denver, have been studied and part of this work is published (Izett and Wilcox, 1982), but other samples could yield additional data if studied with modern methods; volcanic ash beds are key time-stratigraphic markers useful for dating sedimentary deposits and correlating stratigraphic sections in the map area.

New digital geologic mapping of selected areas within the Republican River watershed in Nebraska and Kansas will focus on better defining geologic deposits in the surface and subsurface that affect groundwater-surface water interactions and flow. Specifically, Quaternary fluvial and eolian deposits will be mapped from the surface into the subsurface, and Cretaceous sedimentary bedrock and Miocene Ogallala Formation will be mapped from lower contacts upward; this strategy will allow definition of the unmapped Pliocene (5–2.6 Ma) and pre-Wisconsin (2.6 Ma–>130 ka) alluvial deposits that contain (together with the Ogallala Formation) the principal groundwater resources of the Republican River watershed. Souders (2000), Diffendal and others (2008), and Johnson and Arbogast (1993) provide good examples of modern geologic maps that combine this type of surface and subsurface geologic data. Compilation of existing geologic mapping along the Republican River will be the first stage of this work. Later, more detailed mapping will focus on the highest priority areas of the Republican River and adjoining Platte River. The KGS recently completed new mapping of the Ogallala part of the High Plains aquifer in western Kansas that contours the Ogallala aquifer thickness and elevation (Macfarlane and Wilson, 2006). Similar data exist for the Republican River watershed in Nebraska, but have not been evaluated or published. We plan to work on these data sets in collaboration with the USGS NEWSC, UNL CSD, KGS, and USGS KSWSC. Our mapping will provide a fundamental data set for groundwater models of this part of the High Plains aquifer.

Communication Plan

This hydrogeologic framework task is being done in collaboration and/or coordinated with a number of other scientific entities (USGS NEWSC, UNL CSD, several Nebraska NRDs, KGS, and USGS KSWSC), and the task leader will communicate frequently with them about research activities. Project results will be communicated through reports of scientific investigations, which may include: airborne, surface, and/or subsurface geophysics; Quaternary tephrochronology; and maps and cross-sections relating bedrock and surficial geology to High Plains aquifer hydrogeology.

References Cited in Text

Aleinikoff, J.N., and Muhs, D. R., 2010, Isotopic evidence for South Platte River and bedrock sources for eastern Colorado dune fields, in: Second International Planetary Dunes Workshop: Planetary Analogs--Integrating Models, Remote Sensing, and Field Data: Houston, Tex., Lunar and Planetary Institute Contribution No. 1552, p. 1-2.

Aleinikoff, J.N., Muhs, D.R., Sauer, R.R., and Fanning, C.M., 1999, Late Quaternary loess in northeastern Colorado—Part II, Pb isotopic evidence for the variability of loess sources: Geological Society of America Bulletin, v. 111, no. 12, p. 1876-1883.

Alexander, J.S. , Zelt, R.B., and Schaepe, N.J., 2009, Geomorphic segmentation, hydraulic geometry, and hydraulic microhabitats of the Niobrara River, Nebraska—methods and initial results: U.S. Geological Survey Scientific Investigations Report 2009-5008, 51 p.

Alexander, J.S., Zelt, R.B., and Schaepe, N.J., 2010, Hydrogeomorphic segments and hydraulic microhabitats of the Niobrara River, Nebraska—with special emphasis on the Niobrara National Scenic River: U.S. Geological Survey Scientific Investigations Report 2010-5141, 62 p.

Bettis, E.A., III, Mason, J.P., Swinehart, J.B., Miao, X., Hanson, P.R., Goble, R.J., Loope, D.B., Jacobs, P.M., and Roberts, H.M., 2003, Cenozoic eolian sedimentary systems of the USA Midcontinent, in Easterbrook, Don J., ed., Quaternary geology of the United States: Reno, Nev., INQUA 2003 Field Guide Volume, Desert Research Institute, p. 195-218.

Bleed, A., and Ginsberg, M., 1990, Lakes and wetlands, in Bleed, A., and Flowerday, C., eds., An atlas of the Sand Hills: Lincoln, Conservation and Survey Division, University of Nebraska-Lincoln, Resource Atlas 5a, p. 115-122.

Braddock, W.A., and Cole, J.C., 1978, Preliminary geologic map of the Greeley 1° x 2° quadrangle, Colorado and Wyoming: U. S. Geological Survey Open-File Report OF 78-532, 11 p.

Buchanan, J.P., 1981, Channel morphology and sedimentary facies of the Niobrara River, north-central Nebraska: Fort Collins, Colo., Colorado State University, M.S. thesis, 126 p.

Chapman, S.S., Griffith, G.E., Omernik, J.M., Price, A.B., Freeouf, J., and Schrupp, D.L., 2006, Ecoregions of Colorado (color poster with map, descriptive text, summary tables, and photographs): Reston, Virginia, U.S. Geological Survey, map scale 1:1,200,000.

Chapman, S.S., Omernik, J.M., Freeouf, J.A., Huggins, D.G., McCauley, J.R., Freeman, C.C., Steinauer, G., Angelo, R.T. , and Schlepp, R.L. , 2001, Ecoregions of Nebraska and Kansas (color poster with map, descriptive text, summary tables, and photographs): Reston, Virginia, U.S. Geological Survey, map scale 1:1,950,000.

Cole, J.C., and Braddock, W.A., 2009, Geologic map of the Estes Park 30' x 60' quadrangle, north-central Colorado: U. S. Geological Survey Special Investigations Map 3039, scale 1:100,000.

Committee on Endangered and Threatened Species in the Platte River Basin, National Research Council, 2004, Endangered and threatened species of the Platte River: Washington, D.C., The National Academic Press, 336 p.

Condon, S.M., 2005, Geologic studies of the Platte River, south-central Nebraska and adjacent areas—geologic maps, subsurface study, and geologic history: U.S. Geological Survey Professional Paper 1706, 63 p.

Denne, J.E., Luza, K.V., Richmond, G.M., Jensen, K.M., Fishman, W.D., and Wermund, E.G., Jr., state compilers, edited and integrated by Richmond, G.M., and Coe Christiansen, A., 1993, Quaternary geologic map of the Wichita 4 degree x 6 degree quadrangle, United States: U. S. Geological Survey Miscellaneous Investigations Series Map I-1420 (NJ-14), scale 1:1,000,000.

Diffendal, R.F., Jr., Voorhies, M.R., Voorhies, E.J., LaGarry, H.E., Timperley, C.L., and Perkins, M.E., 2008, Geologic map of the O'Neill 1 degree x 2 degree quadrangle, Nebraska with configuration maps of surfaces of formations: University of Nebraska Conservation and Survey Division Geologic Map GMC-34.

Dreeszen, V.H., Reed, E.C., Burchett, R.R., and Prichard, G.E., 1973, Bedrock geologic map showing thickness of overlying Quaternary deposits, Grand Island quadrangle, Nebraska and Kansas: U.S. Geological Survey Miscellaneous Investigations Series Map I-0819, scale 1:250,000.

Eversoll, D.A., Dreeszen, V.H., Burchett, R.R., Prichard, G.E., 1988, Bedrock geologic map showing the configuration of the bedrock surface, McCook 1° x 2° quadrangle, Nebraska and Kansas, and part of the Sterling 1° x 2° quadrangle, Nebraska and Colorado: U.S. Geological Survey Miscellaneous Investigations Series Map I-1878, scale 1:250,000.

Forman, S.L., Oglesby, R., Markgraf, V., and Stafford, T., 1995, Paleoclimatic significance of late Quaternary eolian deposition on the piedmont and High Plains, central United States: Global and Planetary Change, v. 11, p. 35-55.

Gardner, M.E., 1967, Quaternary and engineering geology of the Orchard, Weldona, and Fort Morgan quadrangles, Morgan County, Colorado: Ph.D. dissertation, Colorado School of Mines, Golden, 224 p.

Hearty, P.J., 1978, The biogeography and geomorphology of the Niobrara River valley near Valentine, Nebraska: Omaha, University of Nebraska, M.S. thesis, 108 p.

Holliday, V.T., 1987, Geoarchaeology and late Quaternary geomorphology of the middle South Platte River, northeastern Colorado: Geoarchaeology, v. 2, no. 4, p. 317-329.

Izett, G.A. and Wilcox, R.E., 1982, Map showing localities and inferred distributions of the Huckleberry Ridge, Mesa Falls, and Lava Creek ash beds (Pearlette family ash beds) of Pliocene and Pleistocene age in the western United States and southern Canada: U. S. Geological Survey Miscellaneous Investigations Series Map I-1325.

Jacobs, K.C., Fritz, S.C., and Swinehart, J.B., 2007, Lacustrine evidence for moisture changes in the Nebraska Sand Hills during Marine Isotope Stage 3: Quaternary Research, v. 67, p. 246-254.

Johnsgard, P.A., 2007, The Niobrara—A river running through time: Lincoln, Nebraska, University of Nebraska Press, 352 p.

Johnson, W.C., and Arbogast, A.F., 1993, Geologic map of Phillips County, Kansas: Kansas Geological Survey, M Series 29, scale: 1:50,000.

Jorgensen, D.W., 1992, Use of soils to differentiate dune age and to document spatial variation in eolian activity, northeast Colorado, U.S.A.: Journal of Arid Environments, v. 23, p. 19-34.

Kellogg, K.S., Shroba, R.R., Bryant, B., Premo, W.R., 2008, Geologic map of the Denver West 30′ X 60′ quadrangle, north-central Colorado: U. S. Geological Survey Scientific Investigations Map 3000, scale 1:100,000.

LaGrange, T., 2005, Guide to Nebraska's wetlands and their conservation needs: Nebraska Game and Parks Commission, 59 p.

Lindsey, D.A., Langer, W.H., and Knepper, D.H., Jr., 2005, Stratigraphy, lithology, and sedimentary features of Quaternary alluvial deposits of the South Platte River and some of its tributaries east of the Front Range, Colorado: U. S. Geological Survey Professional Paper 1705, 70 p.

Loope, D.B., and Swinehart, J.B., 2000, Thinking like a dune field—geologic history in the Nebraska Sand Hills: Great Plains Research, v. 10, p. 5-35.

Loope, D.B., Swinehart, J.B., and Mason, J.P., 1995, Dune-dammed wetlands and buried paleovalleys of the Nebraska Sand Hills: Intrinsic vs. climatic controls on the accumulation of lake and marsh sediments: Geological Society of America Bulletin, v. 107, p. 396-406.

Luckey, R.R., Gutentag, E.D., Heimes, F.J., and Weeks, J.B., 1988, Effects of future ground-water pumpage on the High Plains aquifer in parts of Colorado, Kansas, Nebraska, New Mexico, Oklahoma, South Dakota, Texas, and Wyoming: U. S. Geological Survey Professional Paper 1400-E, 44 p.

Ludvigson, G.A. , Sawin, R.S., Franseen, E.K., Watney, W.L., West, R.R., and Smith, J.J., 2009, A review of the stratigraphy of the Ogallala Formation and revision of neogene ("Tertiary") nomenclature in Kansas: Current Research in Earth Sciences, Bulletin 256, part 2.

Macfarlane, P.A., 2009, New insights into the hydrostratigraphy of the High Plains aquifer from three-dimensional visualizations based on well records: Geosphere, v. 5, no. 1, p. 51-58.

Macfarlane, P.A. and Wilson, B.B., 2006, Enhancement of the bedrock-surface-elevation map beneath the Ogallala portion of the High Plains aquifer, Western Kansas: Kansas Geological Survey, Technical Series 20, 28 p.

Madole, R.F., 1991, Colorado piedmont section, in Wayne, W.J., and others, Quaternary geology of the northern Great Plains, in Morrison, R.B., ed., Quaternary nonglacial geology; conterminous U.S.: Boulder, Colorado, Geological Society of America, v. K-2, p. 456–462.

Madole, R.F., 1994, Stratigraphic evidence of desertification in the west-central Great Plains within the past 1000 yrs: Geology, v. 22, p. 483-486.

Madole, R.F., 1995, Spatial and temporal patterns of late Quaternary eolian deposition, eastern Colorado, U.S.A.: Quaternary Science Reviews, v. 14, p. 155-177.

Madole, R.F., VanSistine, D.P., and Michael, J.A., 2005, Distribution of late Quaternary wind-deposited sand in eastern Colorado: U.S. Geological Survey Scientific Investigations Map 2875, scale 1:700,000.

Mason, J.A., Miao, X., Hanson, P.R., Johnson, W.C., Jacobs, P.M., and Goble, R J., 2008, Loess record of the Pleistocene-Holocene transition on the northern and central Great Plains, USA: Quaternary Science Reviews, v. 27, p. 1772-1783.

Mason, J.A., Swinehart, J.B., Goble, R.J., and Loope, D.B., 2004, Late-Holocene dune activity linked to hydrological drought, Nebraska Sand Hills, USA: The Holocene, v. 14, no. 2, p. 209-217.

Mason, J.P. Swinehart, J.B., and Loope, D.B., 1997, Holocene history of lacustrine and marsh sediments in a dune-blocked drainage, southwestern Nebraska Sand Hills: Journal of Palaeolimnology v. 17, p. 67-83.

McFaul, M., Traugh, K.L., Smith, G.D., Doering, W., and Zier, C.J., 1994, Geoarchaeologic analysis of South Platte River terraces---Kersey, Colorado: Geoarchaeology, v. 9, no. 5, p. 345-374.

McMahon, P.B., Dennehy, K.F., Bruce, B.W., Gurdak, J.J., and Qi, S.L., 2007, Water-quality assessment of the High Plains aquifer, 1999–2004: U. S. Geological Survey Professional Paper 1749, 136 p.

Miao, X., Mason, J.A., Swinehart, J.B., Loope, D.B., Hanson, P.R., Goble, R.J., and Liu, X., 2007, A 10,000 year record of dune activity, dust storms, and severe drought in the central Great Plains: Geology, v. 35, no. 2, p. 119-122.

Miller, R.D., Van Horn, R., Dobrovolny, E., and Buck, L.P., 1964, Geology of Franklin, Webster, and Nuckolls Counties, Nebraska: U.S. Geological Survey Bulletin 1165, 89 p.

Muhs, D.R, Aleinikoff, J.N., Stafford, T.W., Jr., Kihl, R., Beann, J., Mahan, S.A., Cowherd, S.D., 1999a, Late Quaternary loess in northeastern Colorado–Part I, Age and paleoclimatic significance: Geological Society of America Bulletin, v. 111, no. 12, p. 1861-1875.

Muhs, D.R., Bettis, E.A., III, Aleinikoff, J.N., McGeehin, J.P., Beann, J., Skipp, G., Marshall, B.D., Roberts, H.M., Johnson, W.C., and Benton, R., 2008, Origin and paleoclimatic significance of late Quaternary loess in Nebraska: evidence from stratigraphy, chronology, sedimentology, and geochemistry: Geological Society of America Bulletin, v. 120, no. 11/12, p. 1378-1407.

Muhs, D.R., and Holliday, V.T., 1995, Evidence of active dune sand on the Great Plains in the 19th Century from accounts of early explorers: Quaternary Research, v. 43, no. 2, p. 198-208.

Muhs, D.R., and Maat, P.B., 1993, The potential of eolian sands to greenhouse warming and precipitation reduction on the Great Plains of the U.S.A.: Journal of Arid Environments, v. 25, p. 351-361.

Muhs, D.R., Stafford, T.W., Cowherd, S.D., Mahan, S.A., Kihl, R., Maat, P.B., Bush, C.A., and Nehring, J., 1996, Origin of the late Quaternary dune fields of northeastern Colorado: Geomorphology, v. 17, p. 129-149.

Muhs, D.R., Stafford, T.W., Jr., Swinehart, J.B., Cowherd, S.C., Mahan, S.A., Bush, C.A., Madole, R.F., and Maat, P.B., 1997, Late Holocene eolian activity in the mineralogically mature Nebraska Sand Hills: Quaternary Research, v. 48, p. 162-176.

Muhs, D.R., Swinehart, J.B., Loope, D.B., Aleinikoff, J.N., and Been, J., 1999b, 200,000 years of climate change recorded in eolian sediments of the High Plains of eastern Colorado and western Nebraska, *in* Lageson, D.R., Lester, A.P., and Trugill, B.D., eds., Colorado and adjacent areas: Boulder, Colorado, Geological Society of America Field Guide 1, p. 71-91.

Muhs, D.R., Swinehart, J.B., Loope, D.B., Been, J., Mahan, S.A., and Bush, C.A., 2000, Geochemical evidence for an eolian sand dam across the North and South Platte rivers in Nebraska: Quaternary Research, v. 53, p. 214-222.

National Park Service Website, last updated August 19, 2007: *http://www. nps. gov/niob/naturescience/naturalfeaturesandecosystems. htm*

Pigati, J.S., Rech, J.A., and Nekola, J.C., 2010, Radiocarbon dating of small terrestrial gastropod shells in North America: Quaternary Geochronology, v. 5, p. 519–532.

Scott, G.R., 1978, Map showing geology, structure, and oil and gas fields in the Sterling 1° x 2° quadrangle, Colorado, Nebraska, and Kansas: U. S. Geological Survey Miscellaneous Investigations Series Map I-1092, 1:250,000.

Scott, G.R., 1982, Paleovalley and geologic map of northeastern Colorado: U.S. Geological Survey Miscellaneous Investigations Series Map I-1378, scale 1:250,000.

Soller, D.R., Reheis, M.C., Garrity, C.P., and Van Sistine, D.R., 2009, Map database for surficial materials in the conterminous United States: U. S. Geological Survey Data Series 425, scale 1:5,000,000 [*http://pubs. usgs. gov/ds/425/*].

Souders, V.L., 2000, Geologic map and cross sections showing configuration of bedrock surfaces, Broken Bow 1° x 2° quadrangle, east-central Nebraska: U.S. Geological Survey Miscellaneous Investigations Series Map I-2725, 11 p. , scale 1:250,000.

Swinehart, J.B., Dreeszen, V.H., Richmond, G.M., Tipton, M.J., Bretz, R., Steece, F.V., Hallberg, G.R., and Goebel, J.E., compilers, 1994, Quaternary geologic map of the Platte River 4° X 6° quadrangle, United States: U.S. Geological Survey Miscellaneous Investigations Series Map I-1420 (NK-14), scale 1:1,000,000.

Swinehart, J.B., Loope, D.B., and Muhs, D.R., 1996, Dunes, rivers, lakes and wetlands: tales from the Sand Hills of Western Nebraska: Geological Society of America 1996 Annual Meeting-Field Trip #18, Conservation and Survey Division Open File Report Number 52, 39 p.

Thormodsgard, J.M., 2009, Greater Platte River Basins–Science to sustain ecosystems and communities: U.S. Geological Survey Fact Sheet 2009-3097, 6 p.

University of Nebraska-Lincoln Office of Research, 2008, Sustainability in a time of climate Change-- Developing an intensive research framework for the Platte River Basin and the High Plains: Climate Change Workshop hosted by the University of Nebraska-Lincoln and U.S. Geological Survey, May 19-22, 2008, 92 p.

Weeks, J.B. , Gutentag, E.D., Heimes, F.J., and Luckey, R.R., 1988, Summary of the High Plains regional aquifer-system analysis in parts of Colorado, Kansas, Nebraska, New Mexico, Oklahoma, South Dakota, Texas, and Wyoming: U.S. Geological Survey Professional Paper 1400-A, 30 p.

Appendix—Geologic Map Coverage Index

An index of geologic mapping in the GPRB was compiled as a resource for evaluating current status, to help identify data gaps and areas where new digital geologic mapping would benefit ecosystem and climate change research. Mapped areas shown on figure 2 correspond to the Geologic Map Publications section of this report and are intended to illustrate locations for which geologic quadrangle mapping is available. The figure is not intended to reflect data gaps, which involve additional factors such as map scale, map age, research focus, and technology available at the time of mapping and research. For example, not all of the maps listed are of surface geology; particularly for Nebraska, some focus on subsurface bedrock geology and do not map overlying surficial deposits (Burchett and others, 1972, 1975, 1988; Dreeszen and others, 1973; Eversoll and others, 1988; Souders, 2000). In the Republican River drainage, much of the published mapping was done in the 1950s and lacks a topographic base, although new mapping is in progress in a few of the counties (fig. 2).

Recent geologic mapping efforts in the South Platte drainage, published since 2000, have focused on the mountainous headwaters and the urban corridor along the Colorado Front Range (see the Geologic Map Publications section of this report: Widmann and Miersemann, 2001; Thorson, 2003, 2004a, 2004b, 2005a, 2005b, 2006, 2007; Thorson and Madole, 2003; Thorson and Himmelreich, 2004; Widmann and others, 2004, 2005, 2006; Morgan and others, 2004, 2005; Kirkham and others, 2006, 2007; Temple and others, 2007, 2008; Kellogg and others, 2008; Ruleman and Bohannon, 2008; Workman, 2008; Cole and Braddock, 2009; Morgan, 2009), and late Quaternary wind-deposited sand in eastern Colorado (Madole and others, 2005; not shown on fig. 2). Geologic mapping for much of the GPRB in Wyoming has recently been published at a scale of 1:100,000.

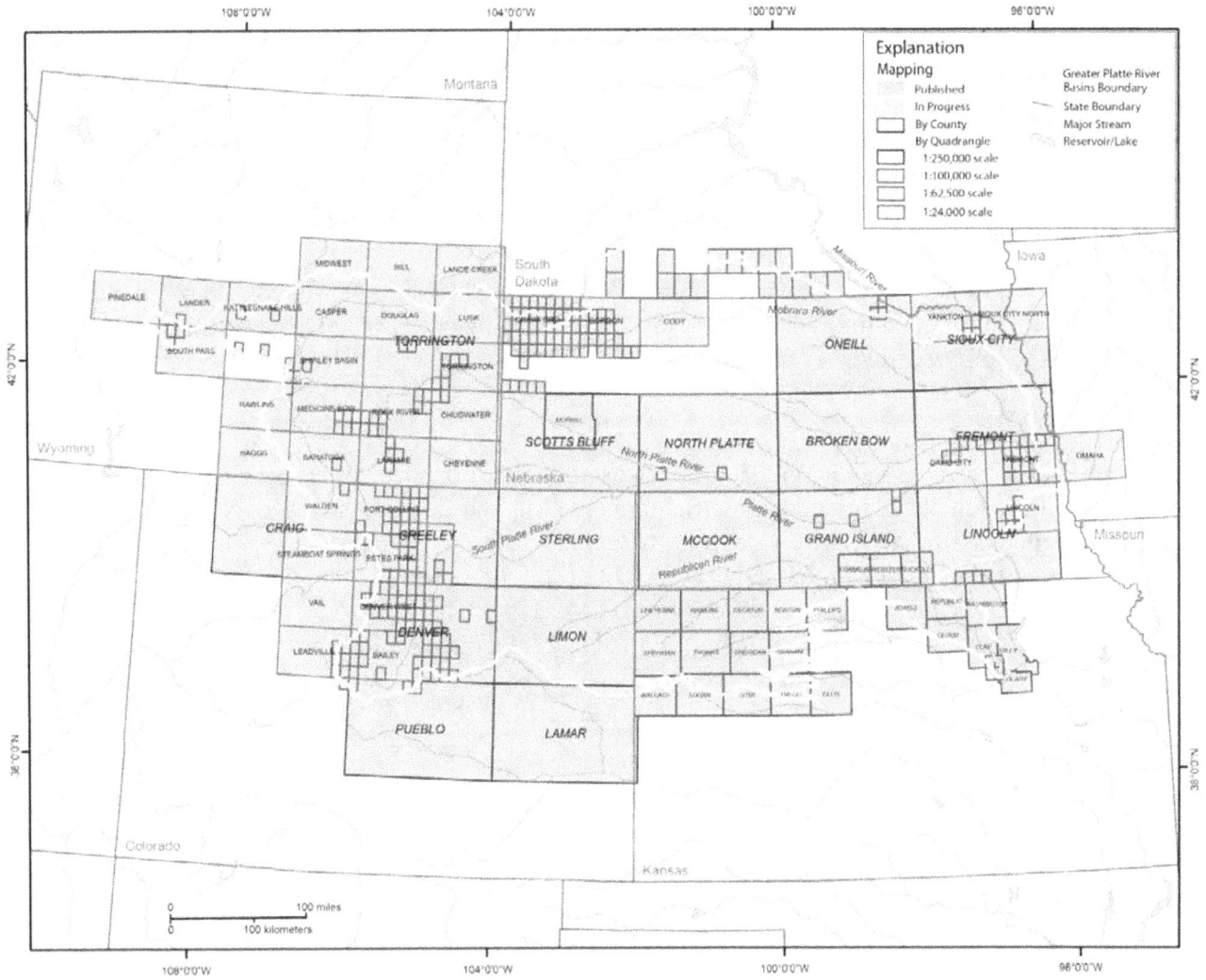

Figure 2.   Index of geologic map coverage corresponding to publications listed below. Only 1:250,000- and larger-scale quadrangle and county maps shown. White areas within the Greater Platte River Basins boundary are areas for which no geologic map coverage was found. Data on new mapping that has either been completed but not yet published, or that is in progress were gathered from State Geological Survey, U.S. Geological Survey National Geologic Map Database, and National Cooperative Geologic Mapping Program websites. Geographic Information System coverage of Greater Platte River Basins boundary provided by Nathan J. Schaepe and Ronald B. Zelt at the U.S. Geological Survey Nebraska Water Science Center.

Geologic Map Publications

To aid the reader in identifying geologic map coverage that might be of interest to them, the names of quadrangles, or in some cases counties, states, or geographic areas covered by the geologic maps, are highlighted in bold font.

Multi-State

Stoesser, D.B., Green, G.N., Morath, L.C., Heran, W.D., Wilson, A.B., Moore, D.W., and Van Gosen, B.S., 2005, Preliminary integrated geologic map databases for the United States; central states; Montana, **Wyoming, Colorado**, New Mexico, **Kansas**, Oklahoma, Texas, Missouri, Arkansas, and Louisiana: U. S. Geological Survey Open-File Report OF 2005-1351.

1:5,000,000

Soller, D.R., Reheis, M.C., Garrity, C.P., and Van Sistine, D.R., 2009, Map database for surficial materials in the conterminous United States: U.S. Geological Survey Data Series 425, scale 1:5,000,000 [*http://pubs. usgs. gov/ds/425/*].

1:1,000,000

Denne, J.E., Luza, K.V., Richmond, G.M., Jensen, K. M., Fishman, W.D., and Wermund, E.G., Jr., state compilers, edited and integrated by Richmond, G.M., and Coe Christiansen, A., 1993, Quaternary geologic map of the **Wichita** 4 degree x 6 degree quadrangle, United States: U.S. Geological Survey Miscellaneous Investigations Series Map I-1420 (NJ-14), scale 1:1,000,000.

Swinehart, J.B. , Dreeszen, V.H. , Richmond, G.M., Tipton, M.J., Bretz, R.F., Steece, F.V., Hallberg, G.R., and Goebel, J.E., state compilers, edited and integrated by Richmond, G.M., 1994, Quaternary geologic map of the **Platte River** 4 degree x 6 degree quadrangle, United States: U.S. Geological Survey Miscellaneous Investigations Series Map I-1420 (NK-14), scale 1:1,000,000.

1:500,000

Ellis, M.S., and Colton, R.B. , 1994, Geologic map of the **Powder River** basin and surrounding area, Wyoming, Montana, South Dakota, North Dakota, and Nebraska: U.S. Geological Survey Miscellaneous Investigations Series Map I-2298, scale 1:500,000.

Colorado

1:500,000

Green, G.N., 1992, The digital geologic map of Colorado in ARC/INFO format: U.S. Geological Survey Open-File Report 92-0507, 9 p.

Tweto, O., compiler, 1979, Geologic map of Colorado: U.S. Geological Survey Special Map.

1:250,000

Braddock, W.A., and Cole, J.C., 1978, Preliminary geologic map of the **Greeley** 1° x 2° quadrangle, Colorado and Wyoming: U.S. Geological Survey Open-File Report OF 78-532, 11 p.

Bryant, B., McGrew, L.W., and Wobus, R.A., 1981, Geologic map of the **Denver** 1° x 2° quadrangle, north-central Colorado: U.S. Geological Survey Miscellaneous Investigations Series Map I-1163.

Moore, D.W. , Straub, A.W. , Berry, M.E., Baker, M.L., and Brandt, T.R., 2001, Generalized surficial geologic map of the **Denver** 1° x 2° quadrangle, Colorado: U.S. Geological Survey Miscellaneous Field Studies Map MF-2347, 27 p.

Moore, D.W., Straub, A.W., Berry, M.E., Baker, M.L., and Brandt, T.R., 2002, Generalized surficial geologic map of the **Pueblo** 1° x 2° Quadrangle, Colorado: U.S. Geological Survey Miscellaneous Field Studies Map MF-2388.

Scott, G.R., 1978, Map showing geology, structure, and oil and gas fields in the **Sterling** 1° x 2° quadrangle, Colorado, Nebraska, and Kansas: U.S. Geological Survey Miscellaneous Investigations Series Map I-1092, 1:250,000.

Scott, G.R., 1982, Paleovalley and geologic map of northeastern Colorado: U. S. Geological Survey Miscellaneous Investigations Series Map I-1378, scale 1:250,000. [**Sterling**]

Scott, G.R., Taylor, R.B., Epis, R.C., and Wobus, R.A., 1978, Geologic map of the **Pueblo** 1° x 2° quadrangle, south-central Colorado: U.S. Geological Survey Miscellaneous Investigations Series Map I-1022, 1:250,000.

Sharps, J.A., 1976, Geologic map of the **Lamar** quadrangle, Colorado and Kansas: U.S. Geological Survey Miscellaneous Investigations Series Map I-0944, scale 1:250,000.

Sharps, J.A., 1980, Geologic map of the **Limon** 1° x 2° quadrangle, Colorado and Kansas: U.S. Geological Survey Miscellaneous Investigations Series Map I-1250, scale 1:250,000.

Tweto, O., compiler, 1976, Geologic map of the **Craig** 1° x 2° quadrangle, northwestern Colorado: U.S. Geological Survey Miscellaneous Investigations Series Report I-972, scale 1:250,000.

1:100,000

Cole, J.C., and Braddock, W.A., 2009, Geologic map of the **Estes Park** 30' x 60' quadrangle, north-central Colorado: U.S. Geological Survey Special Investigations Map 3039, scale 1:100,000.

Colton, R.B., 1978, Geologic map of the **Boulder-Fort Collins-Greeley** area, Front Range Urban Corridor, Colorado: U.S. Geological Survey Miscellaneous Investigations Map I-855-G, scale 1:100,000.

Kellogg, K.S., Shroba, R.R., Bryant, B., Premo, W.R., 2008, Geologic map of the **Denver West** 30' X 60' quadrangle, north-central Colorado: U.S. Geological Survey Scientific Investigations Map 3000, scale 1:100,000.

Madole, R.F., 1991a, Surficial geologic map of the **Walden** 30' x 60' quadrangle, Jackson, Larimer, and Routt Counties, Colorado: U.S. Geological Survey Miscellaneous Investigations Series Map I-1824, scale 1:100,000.

Madole, R.F., 1991b, Surficial geologic map of the **Steamboat Springs** 30' x 60' quadrangle, Grand, Jackson, and Routt Counties, Colorado: U.S. Geological Survey Miscellaneous Investigations Series Map I-1825, scale 1:100,000.

In progress

Bailey
Fort Collins
Leadville (east half)
Vail (east half)

1:24,000

Abbott, J.T., 1976, Geologic map of the **Big Narrows** quadrangle, Larimer, Colorado: U.S. Geological Survey Geologic Quadrangle Map GQ-1323.

Barker, F., and Wyant, D.G., 1976, Geologic map of the **Jefferson** quadrangle, Park and Summit Counties, Colorado: U.S. Geological Survey Geologic Quadrangle Map GQ-1345.

Braddock, W.A., Abbott, J.T., Connor, J.J., and Swann, G.A., 1988, Geologic map of the **Poudre Park** quadrangle, Larimer County, Colorado: U.S. Geological Survey Geologic Quadrangle Map GQ-1620.

Braddock, W.A., Calvert, R.H., Gawarecki, S.J., and Nutalaya, P., 1970, Geologic map of the **Masonville** quadrangle, Larimer County, Colorado: U.S. Geological Survey Geologic Quadrangle Map GQ-0832.

Braddock, W.A., Calvert, R.H., O'Connor, J.T., and Swann, G.A., 1989, Geologic map of the **Horsetooth Reservoir** quadrangle, Larimer County, Colorado: U.S. Geological Survey Geologic Quadrangle Map GQ-1625.

Braddock, W.A. , Cole, J.C., and Eggler, D.H., 1989, Geologic map of the **Diamond Peak** quadrangle, Albany County, Wyoming and Larimer County, Colorado: U.S. Geological Survey Geologic Quadrangle Map GQ-1614, scale 1:24,000.

Braddock, W.A., and Connor, J.J., 1988, Geologic map of the **Livermore Mountain** quadrangle, Larimer County, Colorado: U.S. Geological Survey Geologic Quadrangle Map GQ-1617.

Braddock, W.A., Connor, J.J., Swann, G.A., and Wohlford, D.D., 1988, Geologic map of the **Laporte** quadrangle, Larimer County, Colorado: U.S. Geological Survey Geologic Quadrangle Map GQ-1621.

Braddock, W.A., Eggler, D.H., and Courtright, T.R., 1989, Geologic map of the **Virginia Dale** quadrangle, Albany and Laramie Counties, Wyoming and Larimer County, Colorado: U.S. Geological Survey Geologic Quadrangle Map GQ-1616, scale 1:24,000.

Braddock, W.A., Houston, R.G., Colton, R.B., and Cole, J.C., 1988, Geologic map of the **Lyons** quadrangle, Boulder County, Colorado: U.S. Geological Survey Geologic Quadrangle Map GQ-1629.

Braddock, W.A., and LaFountain, L.J., 1988, Geologic map of the **Crystal Mountain** quadrangle, Larimer County, Colorado: U. S. Geological Survey Geologic Quadrangle Map GQ-1623.

Braddock, W.A., Nutalaya, P., and Colton, R.B., 1988, Geologic map of the **Carter Lake Reservoir** quadrangle, Boulder and Larimer Counties, Colorado: U.S. Geological Survey Geologic Quadrangle Map GQ-1628.

Braddock, W.A., Nutalaya, P., Gawarecki, S.J., Curtin, G.C., 1970, Geologic map of the **Drake** quadrangle, Larimer County, Colorado: U.S. Geological Survey Geologic Quadrangle Map GQ-0829.

Braddock, W.A., O'Connor, J.T., and Curtin, G.C., 1989, Geologic map of the **Buckhorn Mountain** quadrangle, Larimer County, Colorado: U.S. Geological Survey Geologic Quadrangle Map GQ-1624.

Bryant, B., 1974a, Reconnaissance geologic map of the **Conifer** quadrangle, Jefferson County, Colorado: U.S. Geological Survey Miscellaneous Field Studies Map MF-0597.

Bryant, B., 1974b, Reconnaissance geologic map of the **Pine** quadrangle, Jefferson County, Colorado: U.S. Geological Survey Miscellaneous Field Studies Map MF-0598.

Bryant, B., 1976, Reconnaissance geologic map of the **Bailey** quadrangle, Jefferson and Park Counties, Colorado: U.S. Geological Survey Miscellaneous Field Studies Map MF-0816.

Bryant, B., Miller, R.D., and Scott, G.R., 1971, Geologic map of the **Indian Hills** quadrangle, Jefferson County, Colorado: U.S. Geological Survey Open-File Report OF 71-0059, 59 p.

Bucknam, R.C., and Braddock, W.A., 1989, Geologic map of the **Glen Haven** quadrangle, Larimer County, Colorado: U.S. Geological Survey Geologic Quadrangle Map GQ-1626.

Colton, R.B., and Anderson, L.W., 1977, Preliminary geologic map of the **Erie** quadrangle, Boulder, Weld, and Adams Counties, Colorado: U.S. Geological Survey Miscellaneous Field Studies Map MF-0882.

Courtright, T.R., and Braddock, W.A., 1989, Geologic map of the **Table Mountain** Quadrangle and adjacent parts of the **Round Butte** and **Buckeye** Quadrangles, Larimer County, Colorado and

Laramie County, Wyoming: U.S. Geological Survey Miscellaneous Investigations Series I-1805, scale 1:24,000.

Eggler, D.H., and Braddock, W.A., 1988, Geologic map of **Cherokee Park**, Colorado, Albany County, Wyoming and Larimer County, Colorado: U.S. Geological Survey Geologic Quadrangle Map GQ-1615, scale 1:24,000.

Gable, D.J., 1969, Geologic map of the **Nederland** quadrangle, Boulder and Gilpin Counties, Colorado: U.S. Geological Survey Geologic Quadrangle Map GQ-0833.

Gable, D.J., 1972, Geologic map of the **Tungsten** quadrangle, Boulder, Gilpin, and Jefferson Counties, Colorado: U.S. Geological Survey Geologic Quadrangle Map GQ-0978.

Gable, D.J., 1980, Geologic map of the **Gold Hill** quadrangle, Boulder County, Colorado: U.S. Geological Survey Geologic Quadrangle Map GQ-1525.

Gable, D.J., and Madole, R.F., 1976, Geologic map of the **Ward** quadrangle, Boulder County, Colorado: U.S. Geological Survey Geologic Quadrangle Map GQ-1277.

Gardner, M.E., 1967, Quaternary and engineering geology of the **Orchard**, **Weldona**, and **Fort Morgan** quadrangles, Morgan County, Colorado: Ph.D. dissertation, Colorado School of Mines, Golden, 224 p.

Kellogg, K.S., Ruleman, C.A., Shroba, R.R., and Braddock, W.A., 2008, Geologic map of the **Clark Peak** Quadrangle, Jackson and Larimer Counties, Colorado: U.S. Geological Survey Scientific Investigations Map 3010, scale 1:24,000.

Kinney, D.M., 1971, Preliminary geologic map of the southwest third of **Kings Canyon** quadrangle, North Park, Jackson County, Colorado: U.S. Geological Survey Open-File Report OF 71-0171.

Kirkham, R., Houck, K., Lindsay, N., and Keller, S., 2007, Geologic map of the **Garo** quadrangle, Park County, Colorado: Colorado Geological Survey Open-File Report 07-06, scale 1:24,000.

Kirkham, R.M., Keller, J.W., Houck, K.J., and Lindsay, N.L., 2006, Geologic map of the **Fairplay East** quadrangle, Park County, Colorado: Colorado Geological Survey Open-File Report 06-09.

Lindvall, R.M., 1978, Geologic map of the **Fort Logan** quadrangle, Jefferson, Denver, and Arapahoe Counties, Colorado: U.S. Geological Survey Geologic Quadrangle Map GQ-1427.

Lindvall, R.M., 1979, Geologic map of the **Arvada** quadrangle, Adams, Denver, and Jefferson Counties, Colorado: U.S. Geological Survey Geologic Quadrangle Map GQ-1453.

Lindvall, R.M., 1980, Geologic map of the **Commerce City** quadrangle, Adams and Denver Counties, Colorado: U.S. Geological Survey Geologic Quadrangle Map GQ-1541.

Lindvall, R.M., 1983, Geologic map of the **Sable** quadrangle, Adams and Denver Counties, Colorado: U.S. Geological Survey Geologic Quadrangle Map GQ-1567.

Machette, M.N., 1977, Geologic map of the **Lafayette** quadrangle, Adams, Boulder, and Jefferson Counties, Colorado: U.S. Geological Survey Geologic Quadrangle Map GQ-1392.

Madole, R.F., Braddock, W.A., and Colton, R.B., 1998, Geologic map of the **Hygiene** quadrangle, Boulder County, Colorado: U.S. Geological Survey Geologic Quadrangle Map GQ-1772.

Maberry, J.O., and Lindvall, R.M., 1972, Geologic map of the **Parker** quadrangle, Arapahoe and Douglas Counties, Colorado: U.S. Geological Survey Miscellaneous Investigations Series I-0770-A.

Maberry, J.O., and Lindvall, R.M., 1977, Geologic map of the **Highlands Ranch** quadrangle, Arapahoe and Douglas Counties, Colorado: U.S. Geological Survey Geologic Quadrangle Map GQ-1413.

Miller, R.D., and Bryant, B., 1976, Engineering geologic map of the **Indian Hills** quadrangle, Jefferson County, Colorado: U. S. Geological Survey Miscellaneous Investigations Series Report I-0980.

Morgan, M.L., 2009, Geologic map of the **Elizabeth** quadrangle, Elbert County, Colorado: Colorado Geological Survey Open-File Report OF 09-03.

Morgan, M.L., McHarge, J.L., and Barkmann, P.E., 2005, Geologic map of the **Sedalia** quadrangle, Douglas County, Colorado: Colorado Geological Survey Open-File Report OF 05-06.

Morgan, M.L., Temple, J., Grizzell, M.T., and Barkmann, P.E., 2004, Geologic map of the **Dawson Butte** quadrangle, Douglas County, Colorado: Colorado Geological Survey Open-File Report OF 04-07.

Nesse, W.D., and Braddock, W.A., 1989, Geologic map of the **Pingree Park** quadrangle, Larimer County, Colorado: U.S. Geological Survey Geologic Quadrangle Map GQ-1622, scale 1:24,000.

O'Neill, J.M., 1981, Geologic map of the **Mount Richthofen** quadrangle and the western part of the **Fall River Pass** quadrangle, Grand and Jackson Counties, Colorado: U.S. Geological Survey Miscellaneous Investigations Series I-1291.

Punongbayan, R., Cole, J.C., Braddock, W.A., and Colton, R.B., 1989, Geologic map of the **Pinewood Lake** quadrangle, Boulder and Larimer Counties, Colorado: U.S. Geological Survey Geologic Quadrangle Map GQ-1627.

Ruleman, C.A., and Bohannon, R.G., 2008, Geologic map of the **Elkhorn** Quadrangle, Park County, Colorado: U.S. Geological Survey Scientific Investigations Map 3043, scale 1:24,000.

Scott, G.R., 1972, Geologic map of the **Morrison** quadrangle, Jefferson County, Colorado: U.S. Geological Survey Miscellaneous Investigations Series I-0790-A.

Shaver, K.C., Nesse, W.D., and Braddock, W.A., 1988, Geologic map of the **Rustic** quadrangle, Larimer County, Colorado: U.S. Geological Survey Geologic Quadrangle Map GQ-1619.

Simpson, H.E., and Hart, S.S., 1980, Preliminary engineering geologic map and cross section of the **Morrison** quadrangle, Jefferson County, Colorado: U.S. Geological Survey Open-File Report OF 80-654.

Sheridan, D.M., and Marsh, S.P., 1976, Geologic map of the **Squaw Pass** quadrangle, Clear Creek, Jefferson, and Gilpin Counties, Colorado: U.S. Geological Survey Geologic Quadrangle Map GQ-1337.

Sheridan, D.M., Reed, J.C., Jr., Bryant, B., 1972, Geologic map of the **Evergreen** quadrangle, Jefferson County, Colorado: U.S. Geological Survey Miscellaneous Investigations Series I-0786-A.

Shroba, R.R., 1980, Geologic map and physical properties of the surficial and bedrock units of the **Englewood** quadrangle, Denver, Arapahoe, and Adams Counties, Colorado: U.S. Geological Survey Geologic Quadrangle Map GQ-1524.

Soister, P.E., 1965a, Geologic map of the **Fort Lupton** quadrangle, Weld and Adams Counties, Colorado: U.S. Geological Survey Geologic Quadrangle Map GQ-0397.

Soister, P.E., 1965b, Geologic map of the **Hudson** quadrangle, Weld and Adams Counties, Colorado: U.S. Geological Survey Geologic Quadrangle Map GQ-0398.

Soister, P.E., 1965c, Geologic map of the **Platteville** quadrangle, Weld County, Colorado: U.S. Geological Survey Geologic Quadrangle Map GQ-0399.

Soister, P.E., 1972a, Preliminary geologic map and lignite deposits of the **Strasburg NW** quadrangle, Arapahoe and Adams Counties, Colorado: U.S. Geological Survey Open-File Report OF 72-0353.

Soister, P.E., 1972b, Geologic map of the **Peoria** quadrangle, Arapahoe and Adams Counties, Colorado: U.S. Geological Survey Geologic Quadrangle Map GQ-0875.

Taylor, R.B., 1976, Geologic map of the **Black Hawk** quadrangle, Gilpin, Jefferson, and Clear Creek Counties, Colorado: U.S. Geological Survey Geologic Quadrangle Map GQ-1248.

Temple, J., Busacca, A., Mendel, D., and Sicard, K., 2008, Geologic map of the **Dakan Mountain** quadrangle, Douglas, Teller, and El Paso Counties, Colorado: Colorado Geological Survey Open-File Report OF 08-16.

Temple, J., Madole, R., Keller, J.W., Martin, D., 2007, Geologic map of the **Mount Deception** quadrangle, Teller and El Paso Counties, Colorado: Colorado Geological Survey Open-File Report OF 07-07.

Theobald, P.K., 1965, Geologic map of the **Berthoud Pass** quadrangle, Clear Creek and Grand Counties, Colorado: U.S. Geological Survey Miscellaneous Geologic Investigations Map I-0443.

Thorson, J.P., 2003, Geologic map of the **Black Forest** quadrangle, El Paso County, Colorado: Colorado Geological Survey Open-File Report OF 03-06.

Thorson, J.P., 2004a, Geologic map of the **Castle Rock South** quadrangle, Douglas County, Colorado: Colorado Geological Survey Open-File Report OF 04-05.

Thorson, J.P. , 2004b, Geologic map of the **Cherry Valley School** quadrangle, Elbert, Douglas, and El Paso Counties, Colorado: Colorado Geological Survey Open-File Report OF 04-6.

Thorson, J.P., 2005a, Geologic map of the **Castle Rock North** quadrangle, Douglas County, Colorado: Colorado Geological Survey Open-File Report OF 05-02.

Thorson, J.P., 2005b, Geologic map of the east half of the **Larkspur** quadrangle, Douglas and El Paso Counties, Colorado: Colorado Geological Survey Open-File Report OF 05-07.

Thorson, J.P., 2006, Geologic map of the **Russellville Gulch** quadrangle, Douglas and Elbert Counties, Colorado: Colorado Geological Survey Open-File Report OF 06-08, scale 1:24,000.

Thorson, J.P., 2007, Geologic map of the **Ponderosa Park** quadrangle, Douglas and Elbert Counties, Colorado: Colorado Geological Survey Open-File Report OF 07-04.

Thorson, J., and Himmelreich, J., 2004, Geologic map of the **Greenland** quadrangle, Douglas and El Paso Counties, Colorado: Colorado Geological Survey Open-File Report OF 03-09.

Thorson, J.P., and Madole, R.F., 2003, Geologic map of the **Monument** quadrangle, El Paso County, Colorado: Colorado Geological Survey Open-File Report OF 02-04.

Trimble, D.E., 1975, Geologic map of the **Niwot** quadrangle, Boulder County, Colorado: U.S. Geological Survey Geologic Quadrangle Map GQ-1229.

Tweto, O., 1974, Reconnaissance geologic map of the **Fairplay West, Mount Sherman, South Peak**, and **Jones Hill** 7 1/2-minute quadrangles, Park, Lake, and Chaffee Counties, Colorado: U.S. Geological Survey Miscellaneous Field Studies Map MF-0555.

Van Horn, R., 1972, Surficial and bedrock geologic map of the **Golden** quadrangle, Jefferson County, Colorado: U.S. Geological Survey Miscellaneous Investigations Series Report I-0761-A.

Wells, J.D., 1963, Preliminary geologic map of the **Eldorado Springs** quadrangle, Boulder and Jefferson Counties, Colorado: U.S. Geological Survey Miscellaneous Geologic Investigations Map I-0383.

Widmann, B.L., Bartos, P.J., Madole, R.F., Barba, K.E., and Moll, M.E., 2004, Geologic map of the **Alma** quadrangle, Park and Summit Counties, Colorado: Colorado Geological Survey Open-File Report OF 04-03.

Widmann, B.L., Kirkham, R.M., Houck, K.J., and Lindsay, N.R., 2006, Geologic map of the **Fairplay West** quadrangle, Park County, Colorado: Colorado Geological Survey Open-File Report OF 06-07.

Widmann, B.L, Kirkham, R.M., and Beach, S.T., compilers, 2000, Geologic map of the **Idaho Springs** quadrangle, Clear Creek County, Colorado; descriptions of map units, structural geology, economic geology and references: Colorado Geological Survey Open-File Report OF 00-02, 22 p.

Widmann, B.L., Kirkham, R.M., Keller, J.W., Poppert, J.T., and Price, J.B., 2005, Geologic map of the **Como** quadrangle, Park County, Colorado: Colorado Geological Survey Open-File Report OF 05-04.

Widmann, B.L., and Miersemann, U., 2001, Geologic map of the **Georgetown** quadrangle, Clear Creek County, Colorado: Colorado Geological Survey Open-File Report OF 01-05, 22 p.

Wobus, R.A., 1976, Reconnaissance geologic map of the **Glentivar** quadrangle, Park County, Colorado: U.S. Geological Survey Miscellaneous Field Studies Map MF-759.

Wobus, R.A., and Scott, G.R., 1977, Reconnaissance geologic map of the **Woodland Park** quadrangle, Teller County, Colorado: U.S. Geological Survey Miscellaneous Field Studies Map MF-0842.

Workman, J.B., 2008, Geologic map of the **Eaton Reservoir** Quadrangle, Larimer County, Colorado and Albany County, Wyoming: U.S. Geological Survey Scientific Investigations Map 3029, scale 1:24,000.

Wrucke, C.T., and Wilson, R.F., 1967, Geologic map of the **Boulder** Quadrangle, Boulder County, Colorado: U.S. Geological Survey Open-File Report OF 1967.

Wyant, D.G., and Barker, F., 1976, Geologic map of the **Milligan Lakes** quadrangle, Park County, Colorado: U.S. Geological Survey Geologic Quadrangle Map GQ-1343.

Young, E.J., 1991, Geologic map of the **East Portal** quadrangle, Boulder, Gilpin, and Grand Counties, Colorado: U.S. Geological Survey Miscellaneous Investigations Series I-2212.

In progress

Antero Reservoir
Climax
Divide
Eastonville
Marmot Peak

Other

Braddock, W.A., and Cole, J.C., 1990, Geologic map of **Rocky Mountain National Park** and vicinity, Colorado: U.S. Geological Survey Miscellaneous Investigations Series I-1973, scale 1:50,000.

Hershey, L.A., and Schneider, P.A., Jr., 1972, Geologic map of the lower **Cache la Poudre River** basin, north-central Colorado: U.S. Geological Survey Miscellaneous Investigations Series Map I-0687, scale 1:62,500.

Madole, R.F., VanSistine, D.P., and Michael, J.A., 1998, Pleistocene glaciation in the **upper Platte River** drainage basin, Colorado: U.S. Geological Survey Miscellaneous Investigations Series Map I-2644.

Madole, R.F., VanSistine, D.P., and Michael, J.A., 2005, Distribution of late Quaternary wind-deposited sand in **eastern Colorado**: U.S. Geological Survey Scientific Investigations Map 2875, scale 1:700,000.

Kansas

1:500,000

Kansas Geological Survey, 1991, Geologic map of Kansas: Kansas Geological Survey, Map M-23, scale 1:500,000.

Kansas Geological Survey, 2008, Surficial geology of Kansas: Kansas Geological Survey, Map M-118, scale 1:500,000.

County

Bayne, C.K., 1956, Geology and ground-water resources of **Sheridan** County, Kansas: Kansas Geological Survey, Bulletin 116, 94 p.

Bayne, C.K., and Walters, K.L., 1959, Geology and ground-water resources of **Cloud** County, Kansas: Kansas Geological Survey, Bulletin 139, 144 p.

Fisher, V.C., and Leonard, A.R., 1956, Geology and ground-water resources of **Jewell** County, Kansas: Kansas Geological Survey, Bulletin 115, 152 p.

Frye, J.C., 1945, Geology and ground-water resources of **Thomas** County, Kansas: Kansas Geological Survey, Bulletin 59, 110 p.

Hodson, W.G., 1963, Geology and ground-water resources of **Wallace** County, Kansas: Kansas Geological Survey, Bulletin 161, 108 p.

Hodson, W.G., 1965, Geology and ground-water resources of **Trego** County, Kansas: Kansas Geological Survey, Bulletin 174, 80 p.

Hodson, W.G., 1969, Geology and ground-water resources of **Decatur** County, Kansas: Kansas Geological Survey, Bulletin 196, 41 p.

Hodson, W.G., and Wahl, K.D., 1960, Geology and ground-water resources of **Gove** County, Kansas: Kansas Geological Survey, Bulletin 145, 126 p.

Jewett, J.M., 1941, The geology of **Riley** and **Geary** Counties, Kansas: Kansas Geological Survey, Bulletin 39, 164 p.

Johnson, C.R., 1958, Geology and ground-water resources of **Logan** County, Kansas: Kansas Geological Survey, Bulletin 129, 177 p.

Johnson, W.C., and Arbogast, A.F., 1993, Geologic map of **Phillips** County, Kansas: Kansas Geological Survey, M Series 29, scale: 1:50,000.

Neuhauser, K.R., and Pool, J.C., 1988, Revised and reprinted 1996, Geologic map of **Ellis** County, Kansas: Kansas Geological Survey, M Series Map 19, scale: 1:50,000.

Prescott, G.C., Jr., 1953a, Geology and ground-water resources of **Cheyenne** County, Kansas: Kansas Geological Survey, Bulletin 100, 106 p.

Prescott, G.C., Jr., 1953b, Geology and ground-water resources of **Sherman** County, Kansas: Kansas Geological Survey, Bulletin 105, 130 p.

Prescott, G.C., Jr., 1955, Geology and ground-water resources of **Graham** County, Kansas: Kansas Geological Survey, Bulletin 110, 98 p.

Smith, B.D., and Archer, A.W., 1995, Geologic map of **Riley** County, Kansas: Kansas Geological Survey, M Series 36, scale: 1:50,000.

Walters, K.L., 1956, Geology and ground-water resources of **Rawlins** County, Kansas: Kansas Geological Survey, Bulletin 117, 100 p.

Walters, K.L., and Bayne, C.K., 1959, Geology and ground-water resources of **Clay** County, Kansas: Kansas Geological Survey, Bulletin 136, 106 p.

Wing, M.E., 1930, The geology of **Cloud** and **Republic** Counties, Kansas: Kansas Geological Survey, Bulletin 15, 51 p.

In progress

Geary
Norton
Washington

1:24,000 (in progress)

Milford
Milford Dam
Upland
Wakefield

Other

Fader, S.W., 1968, Ground water in the **Republican River** area, **Cloud**, **Jewell**, and **Republic** Counties, Kansas: Kansas Geological Survey, Bulletin 188, 27 p.

Leonard, A.R., 1952, Geology and ground-water resources of the **North Fork Solomon River** in Mitchell, Osborne, **Smith**, and **Phillips** Counties, Kansas: Kansas Geological Survey, Bulletin 98, 124 p.

Nondorf, L.M., and Schott, R.C., 2008, Preliminary GIS-based geologic map of **Rooks County**, Kansas: Transactions of the Kansas Academy of Science, v. 111, no. 1-2, p. 182-183.

Nebraska

1:250,000

Burchett, R.R., Dreeszen, V.H., Reed, E.C., and Prichard, G.E., 1972, Bedrock geologic map showing thickness of overlying Quaternary deposits, **Lincoln** quadrangle and part of Nebraska City quadrangle, Nebraska and Kansas: U.S. Geological Survey Miscellaneous Investigations Series Map I-0729, 1:250,000.

Burchett, R.R., Dreeszen, V.H., Souders, V.L., Prichard, G.E., 1988, Bedrock geologic map showing configuration of the bedrock surface in the Nebraska part of the **Sioux City** 1° x 2° quadrangle: U.S. Geological Survey Miscellaneous Investigations Series Map I-1879, scale 1:250,000.

Burchett, R.R., Reed, E.C., Dreeszen, V.H., Pritchard, G.E., 1975, Bedrock geologic map showing thickness of overlying Quaternary deposits, **Fremont** quadrangle and part of **Omaha** quadrangle, Nebraska: U.S. Geological Survey Miscellaneous Investigations Series Map I-0905, scale 1:250,000.

Diffendal, R.F., Jr., 1991, Geologic map showing configuration of the bedrock surface, **North Platte** 1° x 2° quadrangle, Nebraska: U. S. Geological Survey Miscellaneous Investigations Series Map I-2277, scale 1:250,000.

Diffendal, R.F., Jr., Voorhies, M.R., Voorhies, E.J., LaGarry, H.E., Timperley, C.L., and Perkins, M.E., 2008, Geologic map of the **O'Neill** 1° x 2° quadrangle, Nebraska, with configuration maps of surfaces of formations: School of Natural Resources Conservation and Survey Division, Institute of Agriculture and Natural Resources, University of Nebraska-Lincoln, Geologic Map GMC-34, scale 1:250,000.

Dreeszen, V.H., Reed, E.C., Burchett, R.R., and Prichard, G.E., 1973, Bedrock geologic map showing thickness of overlying Quaternary deposits, **Grand Island** quadrangle, Nebraska and Kansas: U.S. Geological Survey Miscellaneous Investigations Series Map I-0819, 1:250,000.

Eversoll, D.A., Dreeszen, V.H., Burchett, R.R., Prichard, G.E., 1988, Bedrock geologic map showing the configuration of the bedrock surface, **McCook** 1° x 2° quadrangle, Nebraska and Kansas, and part of the **Sterling** 1° x 2° quadrangle, Nebraska and Colorado: U.S. Geological Survey Miscellaneous Investigations Series Map I-1878, scale 1:250,000.

Souders, V.L., 2000, Geologic map and cross sections showing configuration of bedrock surfaces, **Broken Bow** 1° x 2° quadrangle, east-central Nebraska: U.S. Geological Survey Miscellaneous Investigations Series Map I-2725, 11 p., scale 1:250,000.

Swinehart, J.B., and Diffendal, R.F., Jr., 1997, Geologic map of the **Scottsbluff** 1°x 2° quadrangle, Nebraska and Colorado: U.S. Geological Survey Miscellaneous Investigations Series Map I-2545, scale 1:250,000.

Zelt, R.B., and Patton, E.J., 1995, Isopachs of Quaternary deposits, **Fremont** 1° x 2° quadrangle and part of Omaha quadrangle, Nebraska, digitized from a published 1:250,000-scale geologic map: U.S. Geological Survey OFR 95-0721, scale 1:250,000.

1:100,000

Shroba, R.R., Brandt, T.R., Blossom, J.C., 2001, Surficial geologic map of the greater **Omaha** area, Nebraska and Iowa, U.S. Geological Survey Miscellaneous Field Studies Map MF-2391, scale 1:100,000.

In progress

Cody
Crawford
David City
Fremont
Gordon
Lincoln
Sioux City North
Yankton

1:62,500

Swinehart, J.B., Diffendal, R.F., Jr., Swisher, C.C., III, 1995, Geologic map of **Morrill** County, Nebraska: U.S. Geological Survey Miscellaneous Investigations Series Map I-2496, scale 1:62,500.

1:48,000

Miller, R.D., Van Horn, R., Dobrovolny, E., and Buck, L.P., 1964, Geology of **Franklin**, **Webster**, and **Nuckolls** Counties, Nebraska: U.S. Geological Survey Bulletin 1165, 89 p.

1:24,000

(many geologic maps are available online at:
   http://snr.unl.edu/data/geologysoils/digitalgeologicamaps/digitalgeologicmaps.asp)

Condon, S.M., 2005a, Geologic map and topographic profile of the **Elm Creek West** quadrangle, Nebraska: U.S. Geological Survey Professional Paper 1706, scale 1:24,000.

Condon, S.M., 2005b, Geologic map and topographic profile of the **Newark** quadrangle, Nebraska: U.S. Geological Survey Professional Paper 1706, scale 1:24,000.

In progress

Coleridge
Coleridge SE
Denton
Lynch

Marty
North Platte West
Ogallala
Schuyler

Other

Vondra, C.F., Schultz, C.B., and Stout, T.M., 1969, New members of the Gering Formation (Miocene) in western Nebraska, including a geologic map of **Wildcat Ridge** and related outliers: Nebraska Geological Survey Report 18, 18 p.

South Dakota

1:500,000

Martin, J.E., Sawyer, J.F., Fahrenbach, M.D., Tomhave, D.W., and Schulz, L.D., 2004, Geologic map of South Dakota: South Dakota Geological Survey, G-10, scale 1:500,000.

1:100,000 (in progress)

Sioux City North
Yankton

1:62,500

Agnew, A.F., 1963, Geology of the **Mission** quadrangle, South Dakota: South Dakota Geological Survey, Map Series GQ62K-100, scale 1:62,500.

Baker, C.L., Stevenson, R.E., and Carlson, L.A., 1952, Areal geology of the **Herrick** quadrangle: South Dakota Geological Survey, Map Series GQ62K-020, scale 1:62,500.

Collins, S.G., 1958, Geology of the **Wewela** quadrangle, South Dakota: South Dakota Geological Survey, Map Series GQ62K-073, scale 1:62,500.

Collins, S.G., 1959, Geology of the **Martin** quadrangle, South Dakota: South Dakota Geological Survey, Map Series GQ62K-080, scale 1:62,500.

Collins, S.G., 1960a, Geology of the **Patricia** quadrangle, South Dakota: South Dakota Geological Survey, Map Series GQ62K-088, scale 1:62,500.

Collins, S.G., 1960b, Geology of the **Winner** quadrangle, South Dakota: South Dakota Geological Survey, Map Series GQ62K-094, scale 1:62,500.

Harksen, J.C., 1965, Geology of the **Sharps Corner** quadrangle, South Dakota: South Dakota Geological Survey, Map Series GQ62K-101, scale 1:62,500.

Harksen, J.C., 1967, Geology of the **Porcupine Butte** quadrangle, South Dakota: South Dakota Geological Survey, Map Series GQ62K-104 scale 1:62,500.

Schoon, R.A., 1958, Geology of the **Witten** quadrangle, South Dakota: South Dakota Geological Survey, Map Series GQ62K-075 scale 1:62,500.

Schoon, R.A., and Sevon, W.D., 1958, Geology of the **Keyapaha** quadrangle, South Dakota: South Dakota Geological Survey, Map Series GQ62K-069, scale 1:62,500.

Sevon, W.D., 1959, Geology of the **Okreek** quadrangle, South Dakota: South Dakota Geological Survey, Map Series GQ62K-082 scale 1:62,500.

Sevon, W.D., 1960a, Geology of the **Ring Thunder** quadrangle, South Dakota: South Dakota Geological Survey, Map Series GQ62K-089, scale 1:62,500.

Sevon, W.D., 1960b, Geology of the **Spring Creek** quadrangle, South Dakota: South Dakota Geological Survey, Map Series GQ62K-092, scale 1:62,500.

Sevon, W.D., 1961, Geology of the **Vetal** quadrangle, South Dakota: South Dakota Geological Survey, Map Series GQ62K-097, scale 1:62,500.

Stevenson, R.E., 1958, Geology of the **Gregory** quadrangle, South Dakota: South Dakota Geological Survey, Map Series GQ62K-066, scale 1:62,500.

Stevenson, R.E., 1959, Geology of the **Dallas** quadrangle, South Dakota: South Dakota Geological Survey, Map Series GQ62K-077 scale 1:62,500.

Wyoming

1:1,000,000

Edwards, K., and Batson, R.M., 1990, Shaded relief: Digital shaded relief map of Wyoming: U.S. Geological Survey Miscellaneous Series Map I-1846, scale 1:1,000,000.

1:500,000

Case, J.C., Arneson, C.S., and Hallberg, L.L., 2000, Preliminary 1:500,000-scale digital surficial geology map of Wyoming: Wyoming State Geological Survey HSDM 98-1, digital CD-ROM release.

Ellis, M.S., and Colton, R.B., 1994, Geologic map of the **Powder River** basin and surrounding area, Wyoming, Montana, South Dakota, North Dakota, and Nebraska: U.S. Geological Survey Miscellaneous Investigations Series Map I-2298, scale 1:500,000.

Green, G.N., and Drouillard, P.H., 1994, The digital geologic map of Wyoming in ARC/INFO format: U.S. Geological Survey, Report Open-File Report OFR 94-0425, 10 p.

Love, J.D., and Christiansen, A.C., 1985, Geologic map of Wyoming, scale 1:500,000.

1:250,000

Love, J.D., Christiansen, Ann Coe, and Sever, C.K., 1980, Geologic map of the **Torrington** 1° by 2° quadrangle, southeastern Wyoming and western Nebraska: U.S. Geological Survey Miscellaneous Field Studies Map MF- 1184, scale 1:250,000.

1:100,000

Case, J.C., and Hallberg, L.L., 2004, Preliminary surficial geologic map of the **Chugwater** 30' x 60' quadrangle, Wyoming: Wyoming State Geological Survey OFR 04-4, digital CD-ROM release.

Fruhwirth, J., and McLaughlin, J.F., 2008, Preliminary geologic map of the **Rawlins** 30' x 60' quadrangle, Campbell and Weston Counties, Wyoming: Wyoming State Geological Survey OFR 08-4, digital CD-ROM release.

Gregory, R.W., and Micale, D.C., 2007, Geologic map of the **Bill** 30' x 60' quadrangle, Campbell and Converse Counties: Wyoming State Geological Survey Map Series MS-72 scale 1:100,000. [digital also]

Hallberg, L.L., and Case, J.C., 2003a, Preliminary surficial geologic map of the **Bill** 30' x 60' quadrangle, Converse, Campbell, and Weston Counties, Wyoming: Wyoming State Geological Survey OFR 03-7, digital CD-ROM release.

Hallberg, L.L., and Case, J.C., 2003b, Preliminary surficial geologic map of the **Midwest** 30' x 60' quadrangle, Natrona, Converse, and Johnson Counties, Wyoming: Wyoming State Geological Survey OFR 03-5, digital CD-ROM release.

Hallberg, L.L., and Case, J.C., 2005a, Preliminary surficial geologic map of the **Saratoga** 30' x 60' quadrangle, Carbon and Albany Counties, Wyoming: Wyoming State Geological Survey OFR 05-2, digital CD-ROM release. [also OFR 04-10 digital geologic quadrangle map]

Hallberg, L.L., and Case, J.C., 2005b, Preliminary surficial geologic map of the **Rock River** 30' x 60' quadrangle, Albany, Platte, and Laramie Counties, Wyoming: Wyoming State Geological Survey OFR 05-3, digital CD-ROM release.

Hallberg, L.L., and Case, J.C., 2006a, Preliminary surficial geologic map of the **Baggs** 30' x 60' quadrangle, Carbon and Sweetwater Counties, Wyoming: Wyoming State Geological Survey OFR 06-3, digital CD-ROM release.

Hallberg, L.L., and Case, J.C., 2006b, Preliminary surficial geologic map of the **Medicine Bow** 30' x 60' quadrangle, Carbon and Albany Counties, Wyoming: Wyoming State Geological Survey OFR 06-4, digital CD-ROM release.

Hallberg, L.L., and Case, J.C., 2008, Preliminary surficial geologic map of the **Shirley Basin** 30' x 60' quadrangle, Carbon, Natrona, Albany, and Converse Counties, Wyoming: Wyoming State Geological Survey OFR 08-1, digital CD-ROM release.

Hallberg, L.L., Case, J.C., and Jessen, C.A., 1998a, Preliminary digital surficial geologic map of the **Casper** 30' x 60' Quadrangle, Natrona and Converse Counties, Wyoming: Wyoming State Geological Survey HSDM 98-3, digital CD-ROM release.

Hallberg, L.L., Case, J.C., and Jessen, C.A., 1998b, Preliminary digital surficial geologic map of the **Cheyenne** 30' x 60' quadrangle, southeastern Wyoming, western Nebraska, and northern Colorado: Wyoming State Geological Survey HSDM 98-4, digital CD-ROM release.

Hallberg, L.L., Case, J.C., and Jessen, C.A., 1998c, Preliminary digital surficial geologic map of the **Laramie** 30' x 60' quadrangle, Albany and Laramie Counties, Wyoming: Wyoming State Geological Survey HSDM 98-5, digital CD-ROM release.

Hallberg, L.L., Case, J.C., and Jessen, C.A., 1998d, Preliminary digital surficial geologic map of the **Rawlins** 30' x 60' quadrangle, Carbon and Sweetwater Counties, Wyoming: Wyoming State Geological Survey HSDM 98-6, digital CD-ROM release. [also OFR 08-04 digital geologic quadrangle map]

Hallberg, L.L., Case, J.C., and Kirkaldie, A.L., 2001a, Preliminary digital surficial geologic map of the **Lance Creek** 30' x 60' quadrangle, Niobrara and Converse counties, Wyoming, southwestern South Dakota, and northwestern Nebraska: Wyoming State Geological Survey HSDM 01-4 [also released as digital CD-ROM]

Hallberg, L.L., Case, J.C., and Kirkaldie, A.L., 2001b, Preliminary digital surficial geologic map of the **Lusk** 30' x 60' quadrangle, Niobrara, Goshen, Converse, and Platte Counties, Wyoming and northwestern Nebraska: Wyoming State Geological Survey HSDM 01-5, digital CD-ROM release.

Hallberg, L.L., Case, J.C., Kirkaldie, A.L., and Jessen, C.A., 1999a, Preliminary digital surficial geologic map of the **Douglas** 30' x 60' quadrangle, Converse and Platte Counties, Wyoming: Wyoming State Geological Survey HSDM 99-2, digital CD-ROM release.

Hallberg, L.L., Case, J.C., Kirkaldie, A.L., and Jessen, C.A., 1999b, Preliminary digital surficial geologic map of the **Torrington** 30' x 60' quadrangle, Goshen and Platte Counties, Wyoming: Wyoming State Geological Survey HSDM 99-6, digital CD-ROM release.

Hausel, W.D., and Sutherland, W.M., 2003, Geologic map of the **Rattlesnake Hills** 30' x 60' quadrangle, Fremont and Natrona Counties, Wyoming: Wyoming State Geological Survey Map MS-61, scale 1:100,000. [MS-61 also released as digital CD-ROM.]

Hunter, J., Ver Ploeg, A.J., and Boyd, C.S., 2005, Geologic map of the **Casper** 30' x 60' quadrangle, Natrona and Converse Counties, Wyoming: Wyoming State Geological Survey Map Series MS-65, scale 1:100,000. [MS-65 also released as digital CD-ROM.]

Johnson, J.F., and Micale, D.C., 2008, Geologic map of the **Lance Creek** 30' x 60' quadrangle, Niobrara County, Wyoming: Wyoming State Geological Survey Map Series MS-79, scale 1:100,000. [MS-79 also released as digital CD-ROM.]

Johnson, J.F., and Sutherland, W.M., 2008, Preliminary geologic map of the **Lander** 30' x 60' quadrangle, Fremont County, Wyoming: Wyoming State Geological Survey OFR 08-2, digital CD-ROM release.

McLaughlin, J.F., 2008a, Geologic map of the **Lusk** 30' x 60' quadrangle, Goshen and Niobrara Counties, Wyoming: Wyoming State Geological Survey Map Series MS-82, scale 1:100,000 [also released as digital CD-ROM].

McLaughlin, J.F., 2008b, Geologic map of the **Douglas** 30' x 60' quadrangle, Converse and Platte Counties, Wyoming: Wyoming State Geological Survey Map Series MS-83, scale 1:100,000 [MS-83 also released as digital CD-ROM].

McLaughlin, J.F., and Harris, R.E., 2008, Geologic map of the **Torrington** 30' x 60' quadrangle, Goshen and Platte Counties, Wyoming and Scotts Bluff and Sioux Counties, Nebraska: Wyoming State Geological Survey Map Series MS-66 scale 1:100,000. [MS-66 also released as digital CD-ROM].

Sutherland, W.M., and Hausel, W.D., 2006, Geologic map of the **South Pass** 30' x 60' quadrangle, Fremont and Sweetwater Counties, Wyoming: Wyoming State Geological Survey Map Series MS-70, scale 1:100,000. [MS-70 also released as digital CD-ROM]

Ver Ploeg, A.J., 1996, Geologic map of the **Cheyenne** 30' x 60' quadrangle, southeastern Wyoming, western Nebraska, and northern Colorado: Wyoming State Geological Survey Map Series MS-46, scale 1:100,000.

Ver Ploeg, A.J., and Boyd, C.S., 2007, Geologic map of the **Laramie** 30' x 60' quadrangle, Albany and Laramie Counties, Wyoming: Wyoming State Geological Survey Map Series MS-77, scale 1:100,000 [MS-77 also released as digital CD-ROM].

Ver Ploeg, A.J., Boyd, C.S., and Kirkaldie, A.L., 2000, Digital geologic map of the **Laramie** 30' x 60' quadrangle, Albany and Laramie Counties, Wyoming: Wyoming State Geological Survey HSDM 00-1, digital CD-ROM release.

Ver Ploeg, A.J., Jessen, C.A., and Case, J.C., 1998, Digital geologic map of the **Cheyenne** 30' x 60' quadrangle, southeastern Wyoming, western Nebraska, and northern Colorado: Wyoming State Geological Survey HSDM 98-2, digital CD-ROM release.

Wittke, S.M., 2007, Geologic map of the **Midwest** 30' x 60' quadrangle, Natrona and Johnson Counties: Wyoming State Geological Survey Map Series MS-73, scale 1:100,000. [MS-73 also released as digital CD-ROM]

Wittke, S.M., 2008, Surficial geologic map of the **Lander** 30' x 60' Quadrangle, Carbon, Natrona, Albany, and Converse Counties, Wyoming: Wyoming State Geological Survey OFR 08-3, digital CD-ROM release.

In progress

Pinedale

1:48,000

Harshman, E.N., 1968, Geologic map of the **Shirley Basin** area, Albany, Carbon, Converse, and Natrona counties, Wyoming: U.S. Geological Survey Miscellaneous Series Map I-539, scale 1:48,000.

1:24,000

Bayley, R.W., 1965a, Geologic map of the **Atlantic City** quadrangle, Fremont County, Wyoming: U.S. Geological Survey Geologic Quadrangle Map GQ-0459, scale 1:24,000.

Bayley, R.W., 1965b, Geologic map of the **South Pass City** quadrangle, Fremont County, Wyoming: U.S. Geological Survey Geologic Quadrangle Map GQ-0458, 1:24,000.

Bayley, R.W., 1969, Geologic map of the **Bradley Peak** quadrangle, Carbon County, Wyoming: U.S. Geological Survey Geologic Quadrangle Map GQ-0773, 1:24,000.

Dixon, H.R., 1990, Geologic map of the **Seminoe Dam NE** quadrangle, Carbon County, Wyoming: U.S. Geological Survey Geologic Quadrangle Map GQ-1673, scale 1:24,000.

Harris, R.E., and McLaughlin, J.F., 2006, Geologic map of the **Guernsey** 7.5′ quadrangle, Platte and Goshen Counties, Wyoming: Wyoming State Geological Survey MS-68, scale 1:24,000 [also released as digital CD-ROM].

Harris, R.E., McLaughlin, J.F., and Jones, R.W., 2006, Geologic map of the **Guernsey Reservoir** 7.5′ quadrangle, Platte and Goshen Counties, Wyoming: Wyoming State Geological Survey Map MS-69, scale 1:24,000 [also released as digital CD-ROM].

Hausel, W.D., 2006, Revised geologic map of the **Miners Delight** 7.5′ quadrangle, Fremont County, Wyoming: Wyoming State Geological Survey, Map MS-38, scale 1:24,000

Hausel, W.D., 2007, Revised geologic map of the **South Pass City** 7.5′ quadrangle, Fremont County, Wyoming: Wyoming State Geological Survey MS-74, scale 1:24,000 [also released as digital CD-ROM].

Hyden, H.J., 1965, Geologic map of the **Rock River** quadrangle, Albany County, Wyoming: U.S. Geological Survey Geologic Quadrangle Map GQ-0472, scale 1: 24,000.

Hyden, H.J., 1966a, Geologic map of the **Pierce Reservoir** quadrangle, Albany and Carbon Counties, Wyoming: U.S. Geological Survey Geologic Quadrangle Map GQ-0510, scale 1:24,000.

Hyden, H.J., 1966b, Geologic map of the **McFadden** quadrangle, Carbon County, Wyoming: U.S. Geological Survey Geologic Quadrangle Map GQ-0533, scale 1:24,000.

Hyden, H.J., 1966c, Geologic map of the **Bengough Hill** quadrangle, Albany and Carbon Counties, Wyoming: U.S. Geological Survey Geologic Quadrangle Map GQ-0579, scale 1:24,000.

Hyden, H.J., Houston, R.S., and King, J.S., 1969, Geologic map of the **White Rock Canyon** quadrangle, Carbon County, Wyoming: U.S. Geological Survey Geologic Quadrangle Map GQ-0789, scale 1:24,000.

Hyden, H.J., King, J.S., and Houston, R.S., 1967, Geologic map of the **Arlington** quadrangle, Carbon County, Wyoming: U.S. Geological Survey Geologic Quadrangle Map GQ-0643, scale 1:24,000.

Hyden, H.J., and McAndrews, H., 1967, Geologic map of the **T L Ranch** quadrangle, Carbon County, Wyoming: U.S. Geological Survey Geologic Quadrangle Map GQ-0637, scale 1:24,000.

McAndrews, H., 1964, Geologic map of the **Cooper Lake South** quadrangle, Albany County, Wyoming: U.S. Geological Survey Geologic Quadrangle Map GQ-0391, scale 1:24,000.

McAndrews, H., 1965, Geologic map of the **Cooper Lake North** quadrangle, Albany County, Wyoming: U.S. Geological Survey Geologic Quadrangle Map GQ-0430, scale 1:24,000.

McAndrews, H., 1966a, Geologic map of the **Lake Ione** quadrangle, Albany County, Wyoming: U.S. Geological Survey Geologic Quadrangle Map GQ-0508, scale 1:24,000.

McAndrews, H., 1966b, Geologic map of the **Bosler** quadrangle, Albany County, Wyoming: U.S. Geological Survey Geologic Quadrangle Map GQ-0509, scale 1:24,000.

McGrew, L.W., 1967a, Geologic map of the **Antelope Gap** quadrangle, Platte County, Wyoming: U.S. Geological Survey Geologic Quadrangle Map GQ-0619, scale 1:24,000.

McGrew, L.W., 1967b, Geologic map of the **Bordeaux** quadrangle, Platte County, Wyoming: U.S. Geological Survey Geologic Quadrangle Map GQ-0620, scale 1:24,000.

McGrew, L.W., 1967c, Geologic map of the **Casebier Hill** quadrangle, Goshen County, Wyoming: U.S. Geological Survey Geologic Quadrangle Map GQ-0621, scale 1:24,000.

McGrew, L.W., 1967d, Geologic map of the **Ferguson Corner** quadrangle, Platte County, Wyoming: U.S. Geological Survey Geologic Quadrangle Map GQ-0622, 1:24,000.

McGrew, L.W., 1967e, Geologic map of the **Natwick SW** quadrangle, Platte County, Wyoming: U.S. Geological Survey Geologic Quadrangle Map GQ-0623, scale 1:24,000.

McGrew, L.W., 1967f, Geologic map of the **Natwick** quadrangle, Platte County, Wyoming: U.S. Geological Survey Geologic Quadrangle Map GQ-0624, 1:24,000.

McGrew, L.W., 1967g, Geologic map of the **Richeau Hills** quadrangle, Platte County, Wyoming: U.S. Geological Survey Geologic Quadrangle Map GQ-0625, scale 1: 24,000.

McGrew, L.W., 1967h, Geologic map of the **Squaw Rock** quadrangle, Platte County, Wyoming: U.S. Geological Survey Geologic Quadrangle Map GQ-0626, scale 1: 24,000.

McGrew, L.W., 1967i, Geologic map of the **Wheatland** quadrangle, Platte County, Wyoming: U.S. Geological Survey Geologic Quadrangle Map GQ-0627, scale 1: 24,000.

McGrew, L.W., 1967j, Geologic map of the **Wheatland NE** quadrangle, Platte County, Wyoming: U.S. Geological Survey Geologic Quadrangle Map GQ-0628, scale 1:24,000.

Merewether, E.A., 1971, Geologic map of the **Wild Horse Mountain** quadrangle, Carbon County, Wyoming: U.S. Geological Survey Geologic Quadrangle Map GQ-0887, scale 1:24,000.

Merewether, E.A., 1972, Geologic map of the **Seminoe Dam SW** quadrangle, Carbon County, Wyoming: U.S. Geological Survey Geologic Quadrangle Map GQ-1017, scale 1:24,000.

Merewether, E.A., 1973, Geologic map of the **Lone Haystack Mountain** quadrangle, Carbon County, Wyoming: U.S. Geological Survey Geologic Quadrangle Map GQ-1064, 1:24,000.

Reynolds, M.W., 1969, Geologic map of the **Muddy Gap** quadrangle, Carbon County, Wyoming: U.S. Geological Survey Geologic Quadrangle Map GQ-0771, scale 1:24,000.

Schmitt, L.J., Jr., 1979, Geologic map of the **Crooks Peak** quadrangle, Fremont and Sweetwater Counties, Wyoming: U.S. Geological Survey Geologic Quadrangle Map GQ-1517, scale 1:24,000.

Snyder, G.L., and Bow, C.S., 1993, Geologic map of the **Esterbrook-Braae** area, Albany, Converse, and Platte Counties, Wyoming: U.S. Geological Survey Miscellaneous Series Map I-2232, scale 1:24,000.

Soister, P.E., 1966, Geologic map of the **Muskrat Basin** quadrangle, Fremont County, Wyoming: U.S. Geological Survey Miscellaneous Geologic Investigations Map I-0482, scale 1:24,000.

Sutherland, W.M., and Hausel, W.D., 2005a, Preliminary geologic map of the **Keystone** 7.5′ quadrangle, Albany County, Wyoming: Wyoming State Geological Survey OFR 05-6, digital CD-ROM release.

Sutherland, W.M., and Hausel, W.D., 2005b, Geologic map of the **Barlow Gap** 7.5' Quadrangle, Fremont County, Wyoming: Wyoming State Geological Survey MS-67, scale 1:24,000.

Ver Ploeg, A.J., 1998, Geologic map of the **Laramie** quadrangle, Albany County, Wyoming: Wyoming State Geological Survey MS-50, scale 1:24,000.

Ver Ploeg, A.J., 2007a, Geologic map of the **Howell** 7.5′ quadrangle, Albany County, Wyoming: Wyoming State Geological Survey MS-75, scale 1:24,000 [also released as digital CD-ROM].

Ver Ploeg, A.J., 2007b, Geologic map of the **Red Buttes** 7.5′ quadrangle, Albany County, Wyoming: Wyoming State Geological Survey MS-76, scale 1:24,000 [also released as digital CD-ROM].

Ver Ploeg, A.J., and McLaughlin, J.F., 2006, Preliminary geologic map of the **Pilot Hill** 7.5′ quadrangle, Albany County, Wyoming: Wyoming State Geological Survey Open File Report OFR 06-5, digital CD-ROM release.

Zeller, H.D., and Stephens, E.V., 1964, Geologic map of the **Dickie Springs** quadrangle, Fremont and Sweetwater Counties, Wyoming: U.S. Geological Survey Miscellaneous Field Studies Map MF-0293, 1:24,000.

www.ingramcontent.com/pod-product-compliance
Lightning Source LLC
Chambersburg PA
CBHW080350290526
45791CB00009BA/2815